D0038262

HEALING
VICTIMS *of*
SEXUAL ABUSE

HEALING
VICTIMS *of*
SEXUAL ABUSE

PAULA SANDFORD

Charisma
HOUSE
A STRANG COMPANY

Most Strang Communications Book Group products are available at special quantity discounts for bulk purchase for sales promotions, premiums, fund-raising, and educational needs. For details, write Strang Communications Book Group, 600 Rinehart Road, Lake Mary, Florida 32746, or telephone (407) 333-0600.

Healing Victims of Sexual Abuse by Paula Sandford
Published by Charisma House
A Strang Company
600 Rinehart Road
Lake Mary, Florida 32746
www.strangbookgroup.com

This book or parts thereof may not be reproduced in any form, stored in a retrieval system, or transmitted in any form by any means—electronic, mechanical, photocopy, recording, or otherwise—without prior written permission of the publisher, except as provided by United States of America copyright law.

Unless otherwise noted, all Scripture quotations are from the New American Standard Bible. Copyright © 1960, 1962, 1963, 1968, 1971, 1972, 1973, 1975, 1977 by the Lockman Foundation. Used by permission. (www.Lockman.org)

Scripture quotations marked AMP are from the Amplified Bible. Old Testament copyright © 1965, 1987 by the Zondervan Corporation. The Amplified New Testament copyright © 1954, 1958, 1987 by the Lockman Foundation. Used by permission.

Scripture quotations marked NIV are from the Holy Bible, New International Version. Copyright © 1973, 1978, 1984, International Bible Society. Used by permission.

Design Director: Bill Johnson
Cover design by Amanda Potter

Copyright © 2009 by Paula Sandford
All rights reserved

AUTHOR'S NOTE: Names of individuals (with the exception of our son Mark) have been changed, and any similarity between the names and stories of individuals described in this book to individuals known to readers is purely coincidental.

Library of Congress Cataloging-in-Publication Data

Sandford, Paula.
  Healing victims of sexual abuse / Paula Sandford.
     p. cm.
  Includes bibliographical references (p.   ).
  ISBN 978-1-59979-753-3
  1. Sexually abused children--Pastoral counseling of. 2. Adult child sexual abuse victims--Pastoral counseling of. I. Title.
  BV4464.3.S26 2009
  261.8'3272--dc22

                        2009013132

This book was previously published by Victory House, Inc., copyright © 1988, ISBN 0-932081-21-5.

09 10 11 12 13 — 9 8 7 6 5 4 3 2 1
Printed in the United States of America

To John—my friend, my lover, my husband, my partner in the gospel

ACKNOWLEDGMENTS

I AM INDEBTED AND GRATEFUL TO THE AUTHORS WHOSE research has been quoted here.

My thanks to the many who heard of the writing and contributed:

- Some by prayer when they knew the warfare was intense or the needs for energy and illumination were great

- Some by advice and counsel

- Some by recommending books

- Some by granting permission to include their letters or by allowing their testimonies and experiences to be reported

(All names, except our son Mark's, have been changed.)

Special thanks to Mark, who courageously allowed his testimony to be made public, as he said, "for the sake of the Lord and the healing of many." And for his contributions of research and wisdom, especially in chapter 5.

To my husband, John, for his hours of patient editing, suggesting thoughts here and there, and putting up with me while I have been lost for hours at the computer.

To Lloyd Hildebrand of Victory House, Inc. for his consistent prayerful encouragement and competent final editing, and to Strang Communications for their skillful and patient reediting and republishing of this title.

Most of all, my thanks to "Linda" and her two sons for being willing to share their grief and triumph.

And, of course, inexpressible thanks to our Lord Jesus Christ, whose wisdom granted whatever common sense can be found here, whose forgiveness covers my mistakes, and whose grace turns all our efforts into the best wine for the feast.

CONTENTS

INTRODUCTION

Behold, I am going to send you Elijah the prophet before the coming of the great and horrible day of the LORD. And he will restore the hearts of the fathers to their children, and the hearts of the children to their fathers, lest I come and smite the land with a curse.

MALACHI 4:5–6

RESTORING FAMILY RELATIONSHIPS WAS A GROWING EMPHASIS for us during the twenty-one years John and I served in pastoral ministry. We were called to leave the pastorate in 1973 to establish Elijah House as a ministry to serve the Lord in the body of Christ at large. At that time the Lord gave us a mandate to fulfill: Malachi 4:5–6. God's work in the restoration of family relationships became the focus of most of our writing, teaching, prayer ministry, and intercession.

From the beginning, we came to realize that true restoration and relationship involve more than mental choices to forgive and be forgiven, and a great deal more than fleshly striving to be kind and loving. Holiness is not achieved merely by working to order our behavior according to the laws of God. Holiness is a matter of giving ourselves so completely to the lordship of Jesus Christ that by the power of His Spirit living in us we are transformed into His likeness. His purposes, motivations, and responses become ours. Our behavior is then the outward manifestation of what He has been allowed to accomplish in our innermost being.

Many of the people who come to us for ministry are born-again

Christians whose marriages are failing. Many have fallen into adultery; some seem to have no real conscience. The alcoholics, wife beaters, and sexual abusers who seek Christian ministry are seldom the unconverted. They are for the most part those who have made professions of Christian faith. They love the Lord. Many claim to be Spirit-filled. They sit in the church pews, sing in the choir, or teach in the Sunday school. Some even preach from the pulpit. Their common cry is, "I *ought* to be able to live the Christian life! What is the matter? Why do I do the things I do?"

We hear frequent complaints that they know of no one in their churches who will listen to them with compassion and minister to them in depth. Some are afraid to risk exposure and vulnerability by specifically confessing their failures, woundedness, and sins to the people with whom they live and work. A few are more concerned about their reputation than wholeness. But too many have dared to reach out and have come under condemnation and legalistic discipline for being "backslidden." On occasion even the validity of their conversion has been called into question. Or they have seen that happen to others. They feel they would only be chastised and exhorted to try harder. Every day multiple letters and phone calls come to Elijah House from people who say, "I need help desperately. I'm willing to fly across the country to get it. But can you recommend anyone in my area?"

The church has so often fallen short of being the healing, nurturing body of Christ because it does not fully understand the meaning of sanctification. Deep transformation of the inner man needs to happen for everyone in the *process* of sanctification. The apostle Paul states:

> I am conscious of nothing against myself, yet I am not by this acquitted; but the one who examines me is the Lord. Therefore do not go on passing judgment before the time, but wait until the Lord comes who will both bring to light the things hidden in the darkness and disclose the motives of men's hearts; and then each man's praise will come to him from God.
>
> —1 Corinthians 4:4–5

Hidden things in the heart often block us in our Christian walk and keep us from becoming one with each other and with God. John and I have found that when born-anew, Spirit-filled Christians cannot walk the walk in Christ, often what we are involved in as we minister through counseling is the evangelization of the unbelieving *hearts* of believers (Heb. 3:12). (Since inner healing is grounded in a biblical rather than secular philosophy, from here on out I will use the term "prayer ministry" instead of counseling, unless describing secular therapy.)

Many Christians resist the very idea of sanctification as a process. Rather, they see it in terms of a single happening, an experience. They celebrate the fact that their sins have been forgiven and that they are new creatures in Christ, which indeed they are (2 Cor. 5:17), but they ignore the context of this passage, which admonishes new creatures to "be reconciled to God" (v. 20). Many fail to see that the new creature has yet to put off the *practices* of the old man (habitual ways of seeing, thinking, feeling, and acting) and to put on the new self who is "*being renewed*" (Col. 3:10; read vv. 3–15). Many do not seem to understand that they must be renewed in the spirit of their minds (Eph. 4:23) so that they may learn, for example, how to "be angry, and yet do not sin" (v. 26).

Dan was raised in a family that demanded a high level of performance, but affection was almost never expressed; nor were compliments given. Both of his parents worked outside of the home, and he was expected to do many of the household chores and at the same time take care of his younger sister and brother. It seemed to him that he never enjoyed freedom to be with his friends to do the things he liked. And no matter how well he worked at home, there was almost always a harsh word of criticism.

Dan resented the load of responsibility and seeming lack of appreciation, and he projected his anger onto his siblings. They in turn soon learned how to tease and irritate him, but he was not allowed to discipline them in any way. He himself received abusive spankings on a number of occasions when he knocked the younger children around in an outburst of temper. Dan had no positive model or teaching from his parents concerning how to deal with anger; they themselves were explosive. So Dan learned to vent his angers on physical properties. He wasn't allowed to beat up on people, so he kicked doors, pounded tables, threw tools, yelled a lot, and put the blame for his anger on his parents and siblings.

When Dan married, had his own children, and became a born-again Christian, he continued to practice his habit of temper and to blame others for his outbursts. He had neither experienced nor seen another way of handling emotions. There was no other structure built into him. "When I was a child, I used to speak as a child, think as a child, reason as a child; when I became a man, I did away with childish things" (1 Cor. 13:11). Dan's conversion experience did not instantly do away with his "childish ways," and in this sense he had not yet become a mature man. As he was ministered to and taught in the family of God (the church), he was enabled day by day to put off old practices and to put on the new. By this means the Lord transformed him in the process the Bible calls sanctification. He learned to honestly identify and take responsibility for his emotions. By the route of repentance and forgiveness, he was effectively set free from His compulsion to express his anger in destructive ways.

Our renewed mind must be *trained* to take authority over our emotions so that choices to act are not directed by emotion but by the mind of Christ in us. We have been crucified with Him (Gal. 2:20; 5:24), but St. Paul says that we also "die daily" (1 Cor. 15:31) as we reckon ourselves dead to sin and present ourselves as alive to Christ as instruments of righteousness (Rom. 6:11–14).

"By one offering He has perfected for all time those who are [*being*] sanctified" (Heb. 10:14); this passage speaks of a *process*. In Hebrews 12:14 Christians are told to "pursue peace with all men, and the sanctification without which no one will see the Lord." We are commanded to: "See to it that no one comes short of the grace of God; that no root of bitterness springing up causes trouble, and by it many become defiled" (v. 15). We are to do as Paul did: "*I press on* in order that I may lay hold of that for which also I was laid hold of by Christ Jesus" (Phil. 3:12, emphasis added). We are to "*grow* in respect to salvation" (1 Pet. 2:2, emphasis added) and "*work out* your salvation with fear and trembling" (Phil. 2:12, emphasis added).

Two of our former Elijah House prayer ministers, Dominic and Cheryl Beralas, had this to say concerning the resistance in many to the discipline of working out the free gift of salvation in the process of sanctification:

> A major stronghold we have faced in many persons to whom we have ministered has been a dangerous kind of passivity concerning their Christian walk. Many of them excuse themselves from simple obedience and responsibility because they are waiting for some special feeling, or experience, or "breakthrough," not realizing that they are masking their spiritual rebellion and lethargy. We have had to spend hours breaking down this passive mind-set and instructing them that the Christian life is a life of *actively* taking up the cross, mortifying the flesh, bringing thoughts into captivity, and fighting the fight of faith.

Christians who do not understand that our positional perfection in Jesus must become experiential have counted their born-again experience as the *end* accomplishment rather than the *beginning* of a new life empowered by the risen Lord and supported and nurtured by life in the family of God (the church).

Such Christians tend to perform as the Galatians did by striving to behave according to standards and rules rather than learning to walk in the Holy Spirit–directed discipline of "digging deep" to allow the Lord to re-lay our foundations upon the rock that He is. (See Luke 6:46–49, where Jesus is speaking to His disciples.) Consequently, "they have healed the brokenness of My people superficially, saying, 'Peace, peace,' but there is no peace" (Jer. 6:14; see also Jer. 8:11).

You may be asking, "How does all this relate to our topic of healing the sexually abused and the abuser?" The fact is that some Christians desperately want to believe that the problem of sexual abuse cannot belong to them, that someone born anew could not possibly commit such an abomination. However, our experience in prayer ministry shows otherwise, because many abusers had accepted Jesus as Lord and Savior many years before they sinned in this area. Some had even served as ordained ministers of the gospel!

Studies confirm our experience. In his book *A Betrayal of Innocence*, David B. Peters reports the findings of a survey done by students of Fuller Theological Seminary. Fifty-five pastors and 112 counselors responded to questionnaires and reported that they had worked with 981 cases of incest. David Peters reports:

The general characteristics reported by these pastors and counselors seemed basically to fit the study profile seen in secular findings. Ninety percent of the reported victims were female. Fathers and stepfathers were the most common offenders (48 percent as reported by pastors, 56 reported by counselors). Fathers were more often the abusers than were stepfathers. In 64 percent of these cases, the incest began when the child was between seven and thirteen years of age. Incest cases reported seldom involved single incidents of molestation. Sixty percent of the cases reported by the pastor and 65 of those reported by the counselors were repeated incidents spanning a year or more. In nearly half of the cases reported by Christian counselors, it was believed that more than one child in the family had been molested. It was also estimated by the pastors that 62 percent of their incest families were "middle or upper class," while the counselors estimated that 66 percent of their clients fell within that category. Such figures make it difficult for us to follow our natural inclination to deny that child sexual abuse affects Christians in this day and age.[1]

In many cases, churches faced with the facts have done their best to minister not only to the abused but also to the abuser. As the Bible says, however, "My people are destroyed for lack of knowledge" (Hosea 4:6), and all too often ministry was too shallow and other sexual sins and difficulties caused further damage to both the abused and the abuser.

Too influenced by the "instant-on" mentality of our push-button culture, Christians have expected healing to take place instantaneously. These people have been totally unprepared to face what *will always be* a ministry involving diligence, perseverance, and forbearance in love and patience until remorse in the abuser becomes completely transformed and his fractured life has been brought to fullness of resurrection.

This book is an attempt to help all concerned with the problems surrounding sexual abuse to come to greater understanding and empathy toward the victims of this sin. It is important to understand that sexual abuse victimizes everyone—the abused, loved ones, and even the abuser himself.

It is my prayer that God will speak through the pages of this book and that, in so doing, He will bring light and hope to you, whether you are someone who has been sexually abused, a concerned family member or friend, a helping professional, or someone who has abused another. We know that in God there is power to forgive and be forgiven, to change, to grow, and to overcome. Until the early 1980s we would have declared this faith to those who were wounded by abuse from our relatively safe position as prayer ministers. Then, when we lost a beloved son-in-law who molested one of his own children, we personally experienced the pain and struggle that beset many of you. We say to you with more conviction than ever before—God loves all of us unconditionally, and He calls us to love one another and minister to one another with that same love. "But God demonstrates his own love for us in this: While we were still sinners, Christ died for us" (Rom. 5:8, NIV).

Chapter 1

EYES TO SEE AND
EARS TO HEAR

Having eyes, do you not see? And having ears, do
you not hear? And do you not remember?

MARK 8:18

There is therefore now no condemnation for
those who are in Christ Jesus.

ROMANS 8:1

We . . . shall assure our heart before Him, in whatever our heart
condemns us; for God is greater than our heart, and knows all things.

1 JOHN 3:19–20

I CAN'T BELIEVE IT!" "HOW COULD I HAVE BEEN SO BLIND?" "HOW
can I ever forgive myself for letting such a thing go on? I left
my child so vulnerable!" "Where was I? How could I have failed
to see?"

Questions such as these have arisen from the bleeding and bewildered hearts of thousands of parents who have just discovered that
their child, who they felt had been so safe in their love, nurture, and

protection, has been sexually molested by one they trusted. There are no simple answers that can instantly take away the pain.

DEALING WITH SELF-CONDEMNATION

As parents or loved ones of an abused child, we must begin by dealing with our own self-condemnation for our failure to be what we so desperately wanted to be and overcome the need to punish ourselves by wallowing in the misery of "what-ifs" and "if-onlys." It is a fact that Jesus bears our grief and carries our sorrows (Isa. 53:4), but we have to *release* to Him the burden of our woundedness, anger, and hate. The first step is to *choose* to forgive ourselves. With the support and, if needed, the coaching of a prayer partner or prayer minister, we should pray, confessing both our feelings and our faith:

> *Lord, I am overwhelmed by my grief. My heart condemns me for my failure to protect my child. I don't know what to do; it seems like the whole world is crashing in on me, and I'm spinning in confusion. O God, I need some answers! I know that in You there is no condemnation at all. I don't know how to forgive myself, but by an act of my will I make that choice. And I choose to trust You to deal with my heart and set me free from condemning self-accusation or any other way in which I might punish myself.*

The prayer minister or prayer partner needs to respond, strongly affirming:

> *Thank You, Lord, that You weep with and for Your children. You have heard this prayer, and Your heart is full of compassion. Thank You for Your forgiveness, love, and healing balm that You are pouring into this wounded and repentant heart right now. (Person's name), in the name of the Lord Jesus Christ, you are forgiven. Receive that forgiveness. Lord, lift off the*

weight of guilt. Bring all thoughts and feelings of condemna-
tion to death on Your cross. Quiet the inner storms, and comfort
(person's name) in this time of fear. Lord, we stand together
in the strength of Your Spirit and choose to put our trust in
You. We invite You to take charge of us and every aspect of this
difficult situation we face. Let us do all things in Your wisdom,
according to Your grace, love, and power.

Following the prayer, we need to walk in a continual discipline of reckoning self-accusation and condemnation as dead on the cross *each time* we recognize that we are *beginning* to entertain such thoughts and feelings. If we do not, the process of healing stops. Each time we can say to the Lord, "Here I go again, putting myself under guilt. In Your name, Jesus, I renounce that and choose to walk in Your forgiveness." And then go on with whatever tasks we have to do.

UNDERSTANDING WHY WE HAD NO EYES TO SEE

Beyond choosing to forgive ourselves, we need answers to the question, "How could I have been so blind?"

> By wisdom a house is built, and by understanding it is estab-
> lished; and by knowledge the rooms are filled with all precious
> and pleasant riches. A wise man is strong, and a man of knowl-
> edge increases power.
> —PROVERBS 24:3–5

The first answer is that we did not want to believe it possible that a trusted friend or loved one, especially a father or stepfather, could have abused our child. If we suspected at all, we probably resisted the idea, feeling guilty that such a thing would even cross our mind. If suspicion persisted, fear of possible consequences of discovering truth overcame our ability to confront the issue. And so we suppressed our thoughts and feelings to the point of total denial. Unwittingly we became liter-ally blind, deaf, and insensitive to reality.

Linda was a lovely, gentle woman whom John and I had known well for many years. Her marriage to Bill was written in tension, dictated by his frequent explosions of violent, unexplainable temper and punctu-ated by her tearful but persistent and often placating attempts to gather the broken but still workable pieces of their home life together for the sake of their children. Though Bill professed to be a born-again, Spirit-filled Christian, he had fallen into adultery numerous times. He had begged for forgiveness and had declared vehemently on each occasion that he was truly repentant, had learned his lesson, and would never fall again.

Finally, when he was caught seducing a teenage babysitter, Linda recognized that he could never change until he dealt with deep issues in his heart. But he stubbornly avoided taking the initiative to submit himself to a prayer minister, even though friends and family strongly encouraged him to do so. It was not until Linda obtained a legal sepa-ration that he relented by agreeing to receive extensive prayer ministry, that being the prerequisite for any thought of reconciliation. John and I had ministered to the two of them from time to time as much as Bill had been able to allow. But we had seen that he was always more interested in patching a quarrel than in truly healing his marriage or transforming his life. Knowing that we were too close to Linda to minister to them with sufficient objectivity, we recommended that they go to a couple we knew who are among the finest counselors available in either the Christian or secular community.

During the ensuing seven months, Bill faced many of the root causes for his insecurities and for his need to defile women. He dealt with a number of basic sources for his anger. His counselors determined that he had progressed far enough to return to his family. For a period of time he was able to manifest the effects of his healing, and Linda for the first time began to celebrate real hope for a stable marriage. It was at this point that Bill decided he could sustain his new life on his own—without counseling or a support group—and the healing process was aborted. He continued to play the role of the new man, making all the right sounds, but allowed no one to relate closely enough to know him or to haul him to account when he began to fall back periodically into former patterns of irritability and temper.

Bill's and Linda's fourteen-year-old daughter, Karen, who had always been a responsible, sensitive, loving child and good student, began to exhibit rebellious, irresponsible behavior. Truancy and unexplained absences from home grew in frequency. Often Linda would arrive home from work to discover that Karen was nowhere to be found. Attempts to enforce discipline elicited angry, defensive outbursts. When anyone invited Karen to talk about her problems, she defiantly rejected every attempt to reach her and retreated into sullen moodiness.

Finally and with great difficulty she came to her mother with a horrible story of sexual abuse. Her father had been molesting her since the time of her parents' separation, which meant that she was being abused all during the time of their counseling and reconciliation!

Shattered, torn, fearful, and confused, Linda confronted her husband. Bill adamantly denied all accusations, claiming that Karen's imagination was running away with her, that she had been unduly influenced by the stories of friends who had been abused. He went on, dramatically playing the role of the injured party. Linda didn't know whom or what to believe. Finally, after repeated questioning, he confessed to having "touched" her "once or twice." As Karen's behavior progressed more and more to the extreme, however, it became evident that he was guilty of much more than he had been willing to confess.

Realization of what had been taking place for years within her home overwhelmed Linda with the force of a tidal wave. She had wanted so desperately to believe that Bill was changing and had so set herself to celebrate every little sign of his improvement that she had shut out the little signals that might otherwise have alerted her to the presence of trouble. Now she had no alternative but to put him out of the home in an effort to protect Karen. If she had not, the state would likely have taken her children from her. She and the children proceeded with family counseling throughout most of the next year and received a great deal of healing from that source as well as through support groups within her church.

Bill received counseling for sexual rehabilitation while serving a term in prison. He and Linda are divorced. She and the children have rebonded, and the Lord is blessing and redeeming their lives as only He can.

EQUIPPING OUR EYES TO RECOGNIZE SYMPTOMS OF SEXUAL ABUSE

A second answer to parental blindness may lie in the simple fact that few people have either the experience or the knowledge that would equip them to identify (in the behavior of their children) the symptoms that commonly result from sexual abuse.

Educating oneself to recognize sexual abuse symptoms "after the fact" might seem to some to be too late and somewhat useless. This is not the case at all. An important part of healing begins as we are enabled to identify in right perspective the painfully mystifying behaviors of our children. As we realize clearly and specifically that their strange, out-of-control, and often hurtful responses proceed from woundedness and fear, we can begin to relate to them easily with tenderness and compassion rather than with frustration and anger. We can seek their forgiveness not only for our failure to protect them but also for many wounds and unbearable pressures we inflicted on them in the blindness of our desperation to rescue them from self-destructive patterns.

Most victims of sexual abuse have worried about themselves and have struggled with feelings of guilt they haven't known how to handle. Children have felt they were "bad"; teenagers have seen the bewilderment and hurt in their mother's eyes and have felt responsible for injury to younger siblings; they may have wanted to stop running, cease punishing, and ask for help but couldn't. An enlightened and empathetic parent can help them to know that their feelings and behavior were normal reactions to the abuse they experienced, that they were not terrible or crazy. A prayer minister can help victims to see these things, but a parent who is an affirming part of the process can lay an effective foundation for reconciliation and rebonding.

An informed parent of an abused child can also help to provide immeasurable encouragement and healing to others who suffer similar heartbreak.

The following lists of symptoms are not intended to be comprehensive or exhaustive. Rather they serve to provide signposts that point to possible abuse. It is important to realize that children who exhibit some of these behaviors might not be victims of abuse but could be acting out other pressures, upsets, and influences in their lives. This information is a composite of John's and my own experiences in prayer ministry that we found confirmed in varieties of written material and in conversations with parents, other prayer ministers, and preschool instructors.

BEHAVIORAL SYMPTOMS IN TODDLERS AND PRESCHOOL CHILDREN

1. Anxiety in the presence of persons with whom they used to be comfortable; being ill at ease around particular people or types of people; for instance, tense and/or tearful withdrawal from the presence of men and boys

2. Sudden unaccustomed fear of bathrooms or shower rooms, or nervous resistance to being undressed

3. Masturbation that exceeds curious exploration and discovery: preoccupation with excessive sexual manipulation or rubbing themselves against chair arms, pillows, dolls, etc.; sex play with other children beyond the normal "playing doctor" games: inserting objects into the vagina or anus, imitating aspects of adult love play. (In some homes pornographic movie scenes will have

made disturbing impressions.) One preschool teacher reported that she had observed several children who tended to group together in a corner of the schoolyard playing a game of pulling down one another's pants. On one occasion she discovered a child trying to initiate oral genital stimulation.

4.   Sleeplessness, disturbed sleep, nightmares

5.   Excessive crying, clinging to a parent, not wanting to leave the house, unusually fearful responses to being left with a babysitter

6.   Sudden personality changes: i.e., a normally quiet child becomes hyperactive or negatively aggressive toward other children.

7.   Excessive and chronic itching and/or tenderness in genital areas

BEHAVIORAL SYMPTOMS IN CHILDREN FROM PRIMARY SCHOOL AGE TO PRETEENS

1.   Decline in consistency and quality of schoolwork: inability to concentrate, assignments not completed, truancy, tardiness, falling grades

2.   Disturbed sleep, nightmarish dreams, inability to sleep; wearing multiple layers of clothing to bed

3.   Decline in energy level due to anxiety, exhaustion, and/ or lack of sleep

4. Fear of being alone with men or boys; avoidance of particular people with whom the child used to be comfortable; withdrawal from friends and activities previously enjoyed

5. Change in eating habits: nervous or distracted picking at food, compulsive overeating for comfort

6. In girls: poor personal hygiene in a girl who normally cares about her appearance (attempting to make herself unattractive)

7. Exaggeration of normal personality traits: i.e., a daydreamer becomes even more out of touch with the world, an energetic child becomes hyperactive, etc.; sudden dramatic swings to opposite personality poles

8. Invention of irrational excuses not to participate in school or extracurricular activities that formerly inspired enthusiasm

9. Sudden inordinate modesty, self-consciousness about the body; fear of restrooms and showers

10. Sudden cessation of conversational sharing

11. Bed-wetting when it was not a problem previously. A child can be so wounded by sexual abuse that he/she suppresses awareness of sex organs, and thus fails to respond to the body's signals that would normally awaken the one who needs to urinate.

12. Increasing inability to relate well to peers

13. Unexplained anger and aggressive behavior

14. Reluctance to go home after school

15. Running away: boys tend more to run by withdrawing. Girls tend to literally run away from home.

Behavioral Symptoms in Adolescents

1. *Running:* A girl may leave school in the middle of the day to go riding with a friend. She may go to a friend's home, fail to notify her family of her whereabouts, and perhaps spend the night. She may disappear for a number of days, fleeing from the home of one friend to another. When she returns, it is with irrational excuses or often with no excuse at all. When challenged, she "can't remember" what her friend's address is, or she "doesn't have a phone." She may exit by a window in the middle of the night.

   She tends to keep company with friends who are several years older than she, and many of the crowd she chooses are dropouts with no responsibility to occupy their time, with no visible parental support or supervision.

   She may take with her no change of clothes, no cosmetics, not even a coat for her periodic excursions.

   When questioned or confronted, her response is evasive and emphatic: "I'm OK. I can take care of myself."

We have observed such behavior in girls as early as the seventh or eighth grades, intensifying wherever molestation continues to be a threat. Usually the abuser is the father or stepfather, though similar responses may be made to avoid someone in the home who is not that closely related.

The victim may have experienced the initial molestation several years earlier. The first violation inflicted the deepest wounding and established a base of confusion and fear. Subsequent experiences reinforce the wounding, even though the child may have learned to fantasize in an effort to shut them out of her consciousness. If the molestation consisted only of fondling, she may have sensed in her spirit the wrongness and uncleanness of the act, but the one who touched her was Daddy (or some other trusted adult). Children are trained not to say no to adults, especially to their parents. She needed to be loved and affirmed. He represented authority. He said everything was all right. But it didn't feel right. She struggled with conflicting emotions and began to manifest avoidance patterns. She no longer wanted to sit on his lap. She resisted his hugs that earlier she had sought. She no longer wanted her daddy to tuck her in at night. She wanted to sleep with her door closed. If her mother worked, the girl would play at a neighbor's house until she was sure her mother had returned home. These changed patterns develop gradually into more easily recognizable running patterns as she grows to adolescence.

The true reasons for an abused child's behavior are seldom obvious. In the story I shared earlier (Bill, Linda, and Karen), it was easy to attribute Karen's earlier rebellious actions to her father's increasing temper tantrums. Teenagers will not stay around to be yelled at if they can help it! In the best of circumstances, neither do teenagers respond as well to the responsibility of chores, rules, and regulations as they did when they were children. Even well-adjusted teenagers naturally become self-centeredly involved in their own world of activity and forget to come home on time. Unfortunately, Karen's behavior was ascribed to a normal process of individuation aggravated and exaggerated by her father's temperament—until it exploded into frantic rebellion out of all proportion to the known facts of the father's temper and tension in the home.

2. Drug and alcohol abuse

3. Inability to sleep: desperate attempts to crowd out anxious thoughts by reading in bed until the early hours of morning; futile attempts to lose self in the sound of loud rock music through earphones; nightmares; exhaustion

4. Inability to concentrate or stay awake in class; unfinished school assignments; failing grades

5. Increasing disrespect of authority; intolerance of normal flaws in adult behavior; spasmodic acting out of parental roles, as if to "show them" how they should conduct themselves

6. Promiscuity

7. Going to bed fully dressed

8. Obesity

9. Pervasive anxiety

10. Self-mutilation; suicidal talk or attempts

NOTIFYING THE AUTHORITIES

When a sexual abuser has been identified, he must *be reported to the proper authorities.* This is not to be understood as taking revenge. In most states it is a requirement of law. It is also a matter of facing facts. Abusers are compulsive and will repeat the crime until the root causes for their propensity to act in such a way have been brought to death on the cross and they have been completely healed. If an abuser is the father or the stepfather of the abused, he *must* be separated from the home until he has been declared safe by those who are qualified to discern. Even then, he needs continuing supportive counsel until resurrection life in the Lord Jesus Christ has been securely built into the fiber and structure of his being. Let the Christian understand that such wisdom and love are for the abuser's sake as well as for the victim's. "The advantage of knowledge is that wisdom preserves the lives of its possessors" (Eccles. 7:12).

There are undoubtedly hundreds of thousands of cases of childhood sexual abuse that have never been reported. What has happened in the lives of those people? I have seen a great deal of what I call "crippled coping" in many we have ministered to. Some who have sought out ministry were already aware that their present problems were rooted in early experiences of molestation. But a large number have come, having only perplexing symptoms. Suppressed memories then spontaneously surfaced in the prayer ministry process.

The following list from an article titled "Long-Term Effects of Unresolved Sexual Trauma" is a valuable and, for us, a confirming diagnostic guide I wish we had discovered long ago:[1]

CHARACTERISTICS OF WOMEN WHO WERE VICTIMS OF CHILDHOOD SEXUAL TRAUMA

1.   Recurrent and intrusive recollections, dreams, or "reliving" of experiences

2.   Generalized anxiety, mistrust, and/or social isolation

3.   Difficulty forming or maintaining nonexploitive intimate relationships

4.   Sexual dysfunction (aversion, anorgasmia [inability to achieve orgasm], vaginismus [vaginal tightness that can prevent intercourse])

5. Chronic depression, self-blame, and poor self-esteem

6. Acute anxiety or depression related to symbolically important life changes or anniversaries

7. Dissociative features (memory problems, confusion, depersonalization)

8. Vague somatic complaints without objective findings

9. Phobic avoidance, often generalized to apparently unrelated situations

10. Diminished self-protection, masochistic strivings, and repeated victimization

11. Identity focused on a sense of "badness" and stigmatization

12. Contempt for women, including themselves

13. Tendency to fear men yet overvalue and idealize them as well

14. Tumultuous adolescence (early pregnancy, running away, substance abuse)

15. Pseudoresponsible, caretaking role applied inflexibly ("parental child")

16. Passivity and unassertiveness

17. History of promiscuity or prostitution

18. Impulsive or self-injurious behavior (suicide attempts, self-mutilation, substance abuse)

19. Chronic post-traumatic stress disorder (emotional numbing, hyperalertness, etc.)

20. Inappropriate guilt, underlying resentment

21. Intergenerational transmission (abusing own children or marrying a man who does)

22. Defection from family's religion

23. History of childhood learning problems

In our years of ministry we have observed all of the above characteristics in people who experienced sexual abuse as children. We have also seen that helping women to identify their hurts, understand and express their feelings, and develop ways of coping are only the beginnings of healing.

Fullness of healing is accomplished by the person of the Lord Jesus Christ as He is invited through prayer to enable forgiveness, to transform the inner man, and to do a work of renewal in the mind (Rom. 12:2). Whether diagnosis is made and healing is begun in childhood or many years later, no one has to be consigned to live in a wounded, crippled state forever. "For I am confident of this very thing, that He who began a good work in you will perfect it until the day of Christ Jesus" (Phil. 1:6).

Chapter 2

THE DEPTHS OF DEVASTATION

*Look to the right and see; for there is no one who regards
me; there is no escape for me; no one cares for my soul.*

PSALM 142:4

*For the enemy has persecuted my soul; he has crushed my
life to the ground; he has made me dwell in dark places,
like those who have long been dead. Therefore my spirit is
overwhelmed within me; my heart is appalled within me.*

PSALM 143:3–4

THE SEXUALLY ABUSED GIRL

A LTHOUGH THEY WERE WRITTEN FOR ANOTHER PURPOSE, the words of this psalm can also accurately describe the inner turmoil of a girl who has been sexually molested. If the one who violated her was a trusted authority figure, especially if he was her father, she feels totally betrayed. If the abuse came from another, there is still within her a fractured ability to trust. She was not kept from the experience either by her parents or by Father God. As far as she is concerned, she was abandoned in her time of need, and she feels completely alone in her pain. If we who love and minister to her are going to be effective in our attempts to bring healing and restoration, we must try to understand the world of intense and confused feelings that has become her prison and sensitively meet her there.

It is not uncommon for people living under complete tyranny of their emotions to come to us for ministry, crying for us to take away the pain of the moment. In most cases not involving sexual molestation, we can successfully direct them to focus on truths that have more substance, stability, and objective reality than what they are experiencing at the time. If a woman is consumed with hurt and anger because of wounding words and actions inflicted upon her by her husband, we try to help her remember that they once shared times of blessedness. We endeavor to lead her to discover that the painful aspects of her present relationship with him do not represent the whole of their history. We minister to her husband with the same intent. Hours of ministry are usually required to enable each one of them to discover roots in their own hearts that may have contributed to their problems. It may take quite a bit more time to bring about full repentance, forgiveness, and restoration. But if either one or both choose by an act of their wills (in faith) to take hold of eternal truths that transcend their feelings, the process of healing is well facilitated. "For with the LORD there *is* lovingkindness, and with Him *is* abundant redemption" (Ps. 130:7, emphasis added). "Indeed, the LORD *will* comfort…all her waste places. And her wilderness He *will* make like Eden, and her desert like the garden of the LORD; joy and gladness *will* be found in her…" (Isa. 51:3, emphasis added).

The tyranny of pain and fear in the present moment

For a girl who has been sexually abused, there is little capacity to transcend the present moment. Her positive remembrances were shattered when "authority" betrayed her trust. The past is now mirrored in the distortion of a million shattered pieces. Because authority can no longer be accepted as sanctuary, hope, or reliable direction, there are no eternal truths to rest in. The abused one is left with nothing to rely upon but the idol of feelings, and her mind works frantically to justify whatever actions those feelings engender.

You have seen their...idols....Beware lest there should be among you a man or woman, or family or tribe, whose [mind and] heart turns away this day from the Lord our God... lest there should be among you a *[poisonous] root that bears gall and wormwood*, and lest...he flatters and congratulates himself in his [mind and] heart, saying, I shall have peace and safety, though I walk in the stubbornness of my [mind and] heart [bringing down a hurricane of destruction] and *sweep away the watered land with the dry.*

—Deuteronomy 29:17–19, AMP, emphasis added

This passage describes a predicament quite similar to that of the sexually abused. The emphatic declaration of the young lady who continually ran away from home, described in the preceding chapter, was, "I'm OK. I can take care of myself." Her false bravado was an example of the typical responses of many who still have cause to fear repeated sexual violations. However, even when the abuser has been removed from the home and has been denied access to visit (except under supervision), the root of fear and inability to trust any authority figure still lives in the mind and heart of the victim. Desperate cries for help emanate from the same heart that cannot trust any help, even when it is offered by those who are sincere, sensitive, and trustworthy.

Such a wounded one may continue to run—*especially* when love and care seem to be healing her heart! When love begins to penetrate defensive walls to cause her to begin to trust, she feels vulnerable once again and is overwhelmed with fear. She thinks the walls of her closed heart are her protection, and she is frightened when love seems to be melting them down. So she runs just when loved ones think she has a chance to be whole again. For that reason she may compulsively find fault with the people whose love begins to melt her citadels. And so the watered land is swept away with the dry repeatedly, as those who yearn to restore her grieve.

The picture is not hopeless, however. We have seen countless people who have experienced similar wounds find their healing, and now they are ministering powerfully to others. The body of Christ needs to understand the need for wisdom, sensitivity, patience, and perseverance in ministry. We must learn to intercede in prayer effectively and, beyond that, to *be there* for the sake of the abused with a quality of love and ministry that can rebuild trust.

It is in this special ministry to wounded ones that the words of Amy Carmichael in *If* take on clear meaning. She wrote, "If I do not have the patience of Christ my Savior with those who are not growing as quickly as I think they should be, then I know nothing of Calvary's love."[1]

Confusion of identity

A girl who has been sexually abused by her father is driven by many confusing factors within the tyranny of feelings that beset her.

First, she experiences a *confusion of identity*. Her problem is much deeper and more basic than the fact that she has been forced into an involuntary usurpation of her mother's role. Her father has related to her in ways that belong only to her mother. Her sense of who she was created to be as female, daughter, wife, and mother has been battered, torn, and twisted at root level. As a mother tenderly holds her nursing child, deep messages of being chosen and cherished are written into the infant's heart. "Thou didst make me trust when upon my mother's breasts" (Ps. 22:9). As bonding happens, basic belonging is established not only with the mother but with the father as well. From him the little girl needs confirmation that she is lovable and desirable as a female. She experienced an increasing sense of oneness with her mother in the days when she was inside the womb and at her mother's breast. Now she needs affirmation from her father concerning her value as a different and separate person. Father has strong arms, a deeper voice, and a rough whiskery cheek, and yet he can be warm, loving, gentle, and tender. If a little girl feels safe with her father, that builds into her a basic capacity to relax in the arms of her future husband.

As a girl grows up, she naturally identifies in many ways with her mother. If her mother's femininity is something to be admired and chosen, a daughter can more easily choose her own. From deep inside she is enabled to open to life with an attitude of "I too am woman, and I celebrate who I am."

As a daughter is nurtured in the relationship that exists *between* her parents, she absorbs sensitivities and expectations concerning herself in relation to men, especially as she observes her father's attitudes and feelings toward women. If her father treats her mother with respect and affection, she identifies herself as one who will someday be cherished and respected by a man. If he takes time to notice and affirm her, if he communicates his pride in her and expresses affection sensitively and cleanly, she will *know* herself to be a treasure. In this way she will be equipped with holy self-esteem and confidence to present herself sexually and in every other way to her husband as a blessing and a gift.

On the other hand, a girl whose father has molested her feels not only betrayed but also intruded upon, disrespected, used, unclean, trapped, manipulated, robbed, and trashed. Her sense of glory, her dignity, and her worth have been stolen from her. She feels like a nothing, a nobody who could never be accepted by the "somebodies"—if they ever happen to find out what has been done to her. Therefore she tends to gravitate toward those friends who represent her lowered, crippled self-esteem. She clings to them as they tell her she is OK. There is nothing in these lowly people to threaten her self-image, for through wounded eyes she sees herself in them and tells herself she belongs.

Guilt feelings

She struggles with tremendous guilt. In almost every case of molestation the victim feels in some way responsible. "I must have done something!" The "something" she did was in fact only to want her daddy to notice and affirm her with wholesome attention. He failed to understand the sacred trust God gave him to protect his daughter as she blossomed into loveliness. He responded out of his own self-centered, undisciplined need for gratification.

She thinks, "I should have resisted more than I did!" But she had been overpowered on at least two counts. First, how does a child success-fully resist an authority figure who is more than twice her strength? Nevertheless, she is plagued by the thought, "Why didn't I tell some-body the first time it happened?" Second, how can a girl deal with paralyzing fear? Even if a verbal threat was not made directly by the molester, a sense of threat was still very real because the victim knew that discovery would be devastating for the whole family. Her sense of guilt is then sometimes compounded by premature sexual arousal and ambivalent feelings. God built us all to experience pleasurable sensa-tions in sex, but hers have become mixed with feelings of nastiness and revulsion. She thinks, "Something must be wrong with me!" That fearful cry is sometimes falsely confirmed in the victim's mind, espe-cially after discovery, by the accusation of the abuser: "You made me do it! I've lost everything because of you!" Complexities of guilt feelings grow as the family breaks apart, as anger and hurt are expressed, and as her own compulsive running patterns continue to compound the anxieties and tensions already distressing the family.

Occasionally we have ministered to women whose sense of guilt has festered for years, unconfessed, because of responsive participa-tion with a man who drew her into sexual activity when she was a child. I remember one case very vividly. In this instance the woman was not coming to us for help but was a member of a small group of which we were a part. We had met and worked with one another for a year or more so that a base of trust had been established. One evening the anointing of the Holy Spirit was particularly powerful, and group members began to confess their hidden sins one after another as the Lord stirred our hearts. One woman began to weep, and her weeping mounted to sobs. Finally she was able to speak through her tears. "I've never shared this with anyone in my whole life! I know that I can share it with you now because you won't condemn me." She swallowed hard and then exploded in grief and pain. "When I was a little girl, my uncle molested me, and I liked it...and I went after him...and I'm *so ashamed*!" The group held her in loving hearts and arms, prayerfully expressing to her the assurance of forgiveness, nailing her shame to the cross, and her isolation was ended.

Whatever the source of guilt—real or imagined, self-inflicted, falsely assumed, imposed by accusation, deserved, or undeserved— unconditional love provides the milieu for healing and transformation.

Anger and the need to punish

Anger and the need to punish erupt from a seemingly inexhaustible source in the heart of a girl who has been sexually violated by her father. The most powerful venom is often directed toward her mother: "Why did this have to happen to me?" "Why did my mother *let* this happen?" "Why did she marry a man like him? Why did she stay with him?" "She *says* she didn't know anything about it—but she *must* have known! How *could* she have missed it?" "Didn't she *care*?" Sometimes her anger is directed at God: "Where was God anyway? I don't even believe there is a God! Why did He have to make my daddy the way he is?" Or at other people: "I *hate* those snobs at school—those hypocrites at church!" "Nobody has a right to tell me what to do or where to go!"

Cry for help

Until feelings have been identified and directed appropriately, and some forgiveness and healing have been accomplished, expressions of anger may explode indiscriminately, requiring little immediate provocation. If such explosions could be translated into a verbal common denominator for all molested girls, they might sound like this: "Does anybody out there hear me? See me? Care about me? Where were you when I needed you?"

Ambivalence

Love/hate feelings become increasingly difficult to sort through. Ambivalence is chronic. One fourteen-year-old girl, Laurie, who had been abused by her father since the age of eight, cried out again and again, "I hate him! I could kill him! I never want to see him again!" Yet, after a pretrial hearing when she was granted her request to speak to him, she gave him a tearful embrace and later said to her family, again in tears, "He has hurt enough. I don't want to see him go to jail."

Laurie expressed the same ambivalence toward her mother. She would participate in intimate mother/daughter sharing sessions, accompanied by much hugging and weeping, and sleep that night like a lamb, having exclaimed, "It's so good to talk. I love you so much!" But within a day or so she would disappear, leaving notes that slaughtered her mother with accusations bearing little resemblance to truth: "You are never there when I need you." "You give all your attention to everybody else." "You are never home." "I'm the only one who ever tries."

Laurie insisted, "I don't have a father," and yet her love for him persisted. As his day of sentencing by the court approached, she wrote a letter to the judge, pleading for merciful judgment: "He has suffered enough already."

The desperate need to be loved

Desperate needs to be loved and chosen place such a girl in a position that is too vulnerable in boy-girl relationships. It is very common for such a one to be preoccupied with sex and become promiscuous. In all of us there is a need to be chosen, held, and loved. Traumatic wounding intensifies that need. A young lady may send out signals for affection, only to find men interpreting wrongly; in such a case she will often endure sexual activity just to experience the holding she craves.

Every sexually molested girl has suffered the loss of her sense of purity, dignity, and glory. She may respond, "It's gone. Why not blow it? Why not live it up!" In most victims of sexual abuse there is a need to punish, and what better way is there to punish than by behavior that defies the professed moral values of those who let her down? She may make judgments such as, "Men are like that. All they care about is sex." And then she sets out to prove her judgments.

It is also possible that a girl may simply hurt so intensely and feel so completely isolated from anyone she ever loved that she will respond to whatever young man seems to promise to care for her only and forever.

Whether he can fulfill that promise or even has such an intention, she is apt to take hold of him and hang on for dear life, doing everything she thinks she has to do in order not to lose him in the same way she thinks she has lost everyone else.

Fear of pregnancy, deep-down weariness, wanting to die, vulnerability to alcohol and drugs (anything to dull the pain of the inner turmoil)—all belong to the world of feelings that rule her.

Laurie, the young lady whose ambivalent feelings were mentioned earlier, came very close to accomplishing her death wish soon after the discovery of her molestation. Her father had been separated from the family, and she, her mother, and brothers had moved out of the place where they had been living. The move was an attempt to provide a new environment where Laurie could learn to rest and feel more secure. Memories associated with the old house had made relaxation impossible.

The move proved to be a disappointment from the start. Memories traveled inside of Laurie no matter where she went. She would lie awake until the early hours of the morning, needing desperately to sleep but kept alert by the tension built into her by her father's repeated nocturnal advances. She tried to overcome her thoughts and feelings with music. She read. Sometimes she even prayed, but no one seemed to be listening. She felt overcome by loneliness, pain, and fear. Often the little sleep she managed to obtain would be so filled with nightmarish dreams that she began to fear sleep itself.

Since she had no ability to trust anyone, all attempts to help Laurie were rejected. "I'm OK. I don't want to talk about it" was the substance of her conversation in the family. Sessions with a court-appointed counselor never progressed beyond the counselor's frustrated attempts to establish sufficient rapport to begin to discuss real issues.

Laurie would leave for school in the morning, fall asleep in class, and then wander away during the noon hour to join some of the school dropouts who "hung around" for lack of something better to do. Her mother was working full-time to support the family, and very soon the unsupervised afternoon atmosphere of her home attracted a growing number of teenage ne'er-do-wells. They came with their rock music, booze, and drugs; they broke into locked storage closets and cupboards, ate everything in sight, and left unbelievable messes as they exited through the doors and windows before Laurie's mother arrived at 5:30 p.m.

Parental confrontive action was not lacking. But the situation was soon out of hand. Laurie sincerely promised to tell the kids they would have to do their partying somewhere else, but she was continually overpowered by her gang, who didn't care and were not at all intimidated by threats. Unable to control them, she began to disappear with them. A few times she came home very late and very drunk. Often she didn't come home at all. Her mother tried and failed in every approach she could think of to break through her defensive walls and win her confidence.

One evening Laurie's mother came home from work to be greeted by several young people who were attempting to help Laurie into a car. "We have to get her to the hospital! She swallowed everything in the medicine cabinet!"

On the way to the emergency room, one of the girls confided that Laurie thought she was pregnant. Pregnancy tests proved to be negative, and a stomach pump cleared out all but her pain, fear, and anger. Laurie's mother had no alternative but to resign her job though financial aid was ridiculously meager.

Mother love and family support poured unconditionally into Laurie during that crisis time, and this planted a new seed of trust in a wounded and frightened girl. The seed had to survive multiple storms that followed, but by the Lord's grace it took root in her and continues to grow.

A SEXUALLY ABUSED BOY

There is very little testimony available to describe the long-term effects of sexual abuse done to young boys. They don't talk about it. Some authorities have attributed this largely to our culture that strongly teaches every male that he must be in control of his situation and his emotions. He is not supposed to be a victim. Some say it is a blow to his manhood to be overcome by another or to acknowledge fear, hurt, grief, or pain. Therefore he tends to withdraw and suppress his feelings, often even the memory of traumatic violation. I agree. Certainly he is admonished from babyhood: "Don't be a crybaby." "Don't be a sissy." "Be a big boy." "Don't let that bully push you around." However, I believe that when a boy has been overcome and sexually molested, it is sometimes also the attacker's threat to harm others if he tells that hooks into an innate male desire to protect those he loves and becomes the most important factor influencing him to silence and secrecy. Suppression of memory then is a way of coping with burdens too overwhelming to carry consciously.

There comes a time when suppression, meant to be a temporary defense mechanism, no longer protects. Rather, the one who suppresses memories of trauma will be driven from deep inside by unseen, unidentified forces. It is not that repressed fear, hurt, grief, and pain will not be expressed at all. Instead, those feelings *will* manifest unconsciously in twisted and misdirected ways. Relationships between root causes and fruits in attitudes and behaviors will be obscured. Neither the victim nor others then understand why he feels and acts as he does. Therefore the victim is left even more vulnerable to confusion concerning his identity, compounded by misunderstanding from others and the pain of rejection, loneliness, and further wounding.

Our son Mark, who is an extremely insightful and effective prayer minister, teacher, and author, suffered the trauma of violent molestation when he was only five years old. We, his parents, did not know, nor did anyone else, and his own memories were suppressed for nearly twenty-four years. This is his story as told to me. I share it with his permission and encouragement so that others might benefit from the wisdom gained in the battles he fought and may come to trust Father God who persists in love until His children are healed.

First, let me describe Mark's personality as we knew him as a child.

Mark was artistically gifted from the beginning. Even as a toddler he had a gentleness about him. When we went on camping trips as a family, little animals in the forest would play around him and eat out of his hands. As he grew, he related to art, music, and beauty in nature with amazing sensitivity. He was often surprised that others missed subtle details so evident to his eyes and was frustrated with people who wanted to hurry on a hike through the woods or rush through a museum without stopping to ponder a work of art.

At an early age his faith was simple and firm. A bishop became ill while visiting in our home. Three-year-old Mark laid his little hand on him and prayed, "Lord, heal de bishop," and the bishop was healed instantly.

A dreamer, Mark would spend long periods of time studying pictures in a magazine or simply sailing off into space. If he colored in a coloring book, he would creatively add to the pictures. When he learned to print, he drew vines, flowers, and elves swinging from the letters. We first counted it as a blessing that he could entertain himself easily for hours at a time. Later we discovered that though some of his dreaming was fun and creative fantasy, much was flight from the jangle and heaviness he felt but couldn't identify in the troubled community in which we lived. A natural burden bearer, he tuned in with his sensitive spirit to what many others were feeling, was sometimes overwhelmed by it, and learned before he was out of diapers to withdraw in order to create his own more comfortable atmosphere. This defensive wrap served not only as a protection from the hurtful "vibes" in the neigh-borhood (we were pastoring a troubled church in a town where there was much rancor), but it also served as a shield that insulated him from the positive emotional nurture that he might have received from family activities.

As he grew up he would sometimes try to share something out of the midst of his dreaming, but for others it was like arriving in the middle of a complex movie. Adults tried to listen. Children shook their heads, laughed, and went their way. On an outing in the woods, Mark might try to call his friends' attention to the exciting gymnastics of a bug under a leaf. But they preferred to crash through the underbrush. Boys threw rocks at frogs. Mark wept for the frogs, identifying with their pain, and wondered why he felt and saw things so differently than the other boys.

As parents we appreciated and valued his artistic and sensitive nature, but quite often we found ourselves anxious because of his seemingly total unawareness of the way others approached life. We tried to warn him, "That's great, Mark, but lots of other people don't think that way. Don't be disappointed if they misunderstand what you say."

In the timeless world his dreaming created, it was difficult to get him anywhere on time. He would pull his socks halfway on. Fifteen minutes later he would still be in the same position, like a catatonic, totally absorbed in his thoughts. On the way to school he would lose himself in the delight of kicking leaves up and down along the curb and wander into class at ten o'clock. Our family, in a clumsy attempt to help him and to spare embarrassment (his and ours), tried to call him to attention: "Wake up, Mark!" "Hurry! Time doesn't stand still for you!" "What are you doing? You don't have to be like other people, but you're a part of this world, and you're going to have to learn to live in it." "Everyone's waiting for you! Get with it!" "Think! How is that going to sound to other people?" "You are going to have to fight to be aware of where others are coming from!" I'm sure we must have affected him like constant rain beating on his face. (See Proverbs 27:15.)

Sometimes someone would unkindly respond to what seemed to be his "off-the-wall-out-of-his-dreamworld" remarks with an exasperated, "Oh, Mark! Grow up!" Or worse, comment to another as though he were out of hearing, "You know Mark." Mark usually endured such verbal lacerations silently—and occasionally with a half-suppressed glee belonging to a kind of passive retaliation for wounds received.

Years later, we discovered that for Mark much of this was due to symptoms of Asperger's syndrome, a mild version of autism that was not a known diagnosis when he was a child. We could not have known that that caused, among other things, his spaciness, exceptionally slow acquisition of social skills, occasional short-circuiting of mind and body (hence, the seemingly catatonic moments), and lack of a sense of the passing of time. But Mark believes that those symptoms were magnified by his reactions to being molested. Molested boys tend to become spacey, withdrawn, and socially cut off. How much more so when the brain was already predisposed that way!

The miracle we celebrate today is that Mark did manage to get to the world on time, without losing either his artistic sensitivity or childlike faith that God's grace blends well with a maturing gift of penetrating insight into the problems of people. Miraculously, God has healed most of the Asperger's traits and continues to heal what remains of it—something science says is impossible! And Mark has forgiven our bumbling attempts to help him and has contributed significant new tools to the ministry of Elijah House, in which he is now spiritual director.

Mark declares, from his personal life and his experience as a prayer minister, "Molestation throws its victims into exaggerations of normal patterns." We can see that now. He was a natural dreamer, more like his father than his father was, and that became an escape from the pain. When his younger brother John was born, Mark appeared to compete to be the little one. We can now attribute much of that to Asperger's, but Mark's tendency to regress was worsened by his need for comfort from parents who didn't know he had been abused. His artistic giftings were far more satisfying to him than the roughhousing most boys enjoy, which felt to him like an echo of the brutality he could not consciously recall. His empathetic nature sometimes caused him to be overwhelmed with burdens he couldn't sort out, compounded by his own burden that no one carried for him. We watched those natural patterns intensify, but ignorantly failed to identify them as behavioral clues that might have revealed to us the fact of the trauma he experienced at age five.

I remember being concerned about a sudden manifestation of acute modesty in Mark at that age. If I happened to blunder into the bathroom while Mark was having a bath, he nearly squirmed down the drain in his franticness to cover up! But when I questioned him and his sister about the behavior of the older brothers of a friend they often visited, both assured me that there had been nothing out of order. They appeared to be telling the truth, and we had always been able to trust what they said. I was disturbed in my spirit at the time, but I did not see how I could push the issue without injuring them by accusations that might prove to be altogether false. John felt an irrational irritation in his spirit whenever he came near the sons of that farming family in our parish. He found he could not like them and wanted to be angry with them, but he could find no objective reasons for his feelings. Today Mark testifies that his experience with those boys was so intensely traumatic he quickly and totally suppressed the memory of it until the Lord brought it to the surface bit by bit as the time was ripe.

The number four was significant in the gradual revelation of truth. *Four* teenage boys molested him. When he entered the *fourth* grade he developed a compulsive habit of counting to *four*. Again and again he would count, "1-2-3-4." Then he would count to four *four* times. He began to experience a daydream he couldn't stop. In his imagination he would see his penis grow long like a garden hose and fly around the classroom, knocking people down and wrapping itself around them. He would frantically try to reel it in but fail. These were symptoms of obsessive-compulsive disorder, through which Mark's buried memory was surfacing symbolically. He was unable to concentrate on his schoolwork, and when the teacher asked what he was thinking about, he couldn't tell her. Again and again she would physically thump him on the head to demand his attention, and the whole class would laugh. He told us only the part about the head-thumping, and we let the teacher know that her method was accomplishing no good purpose, but apparently she had no ears to hear. The abuse continued, and Mark said no more about it.

At age twelve he began to be afraid because he felt himself being physically attracted to boys. He was stimulated by a movie character who was gentle and sensitive but all male. He caught a whiff of man's cologne—how sensuous it smelled! He was horrified even to think about what his feelings might imply and comforted himself with the thought that it was probably only a passing phase. But it didn't pass.

Junior high school became unbearable for Mark in a mining town where sports and the macho image were deified. Being a late bloomer both emotionally and physically, he was small for his age. Had he cared about basketball, most passes would have gone over his head. His physical education teacher called him "Susie" and regularly joined with the guys in the class in making fun of him. One day when classmates picked him up and threw him into the shower, he panicked, and the report spread rapidly throughout the school. Ridicule was hurled at him from all directions. It had been a fairly frequent occurrence for someone to get thrown into the shower. A few other guys had been chosen for that treatment at one time or another and had laughed about it. No one had any way of knowing that to Mark it was a parallel to his childhood molestation and triggered the panic he had felt when he was overpowered then. Mark himself couldn't understand why he reacted the way he did and was embarrassed and humiliated.

At age thirteen he began to think a lot about suicide. Harassment from the boys across the street was so intense and hurtful that twice Mark carried a steak knife to school in his pocket, intending to stab one of them at the onset of trouble. The first time he carried the knife, his foremost antagonist was absent; on the next occasion he was shockingly friendly, and Mark didn't have the heart to attack him for past sins. He maintains that he probably would not have actually carried out his intent had he been provoked, but compelling anger certainly corrupted his emotions.

By the time Mark was fourteen, life was so tension-filled that masturbation became a frequent release and compulsive problem. At first he felt he might go to hell if he continued, but it became impossible to stop. Teenage identity crisis for him was megasized. He was always horrified of boys who demonstrated any kind of roughhousing. Rough behavior was the daily fare at the high school—in the halls, the gym, and especially in the men's washroom (where ambush was regularly laid to de-pants the unsuspecting, and many were baptized head-in-toilet or placed upside down in the nearest trash can). It seemed brutal and incredibly ugly, and he despised it. Girls had it so good. They could occupy themselves quietly as they pleased and look pretty. He wished he were one and was manifesting increasingly effeminate mannerisms. One day he told me that he didn't want to be a man. He remembers my response, "Well, you *are*—and you'll have to live with it."

Mark also remembers his father's exasperation: "Dad said he was considering making me go into the army 'to make a man' of me. When I refused, he said he would make it like the army at the house and would ride me like a drill sergeant. Loren helped out by making me run stairs, and Johnny and Tim snickered as I went by. You [mother] also agreed to this. I think subconsciously I must have seen a parallel with being ganged up on at an earlier age. That, and the threat of the army [remember, this was the Vietnam era], confirmed my impression at the time that masculinity stood for all that is grotesque, that it stamped people by force into its mold."

I remember driving Mark somewhere in the car one afternoon. He called a friendly "Hi" to a girl who was walking along the street, and she responded with a cruel derogative, "Fag." His eyes brimmed with tears; he wasn't able to talk about it or release his hurt or receive more than a little of the comfort I offered.

Before Mark graduated, he was asked to paint a mural to cover a large portion of a wall of the high school auditorium. He produced a magnificent work of art that drew admiration and compliments from many of the faculty and students. They were pleased by the beauty of a female figure with long hair flowing in the wind. Her hand held the light fixture as a torch, and coming from the area of her face and across the wall were—something like leaves? Or tears? Everyone wondered. Mark shared only with his family that he had painted "Wisdom Weeping Over the School," his covert manner of expressing the anger he would not allow in more conventional teenage ways.

During Mark's college years his sexual feelings and fears were suppressed as studies and work demanded thought, time, and energies. He initiated and sustained (to this day) a discipline of bodybuilding that produced a magnificently muscular physique. The ninety-seven-pound weakling had now become an Atlas. "Vacation" times were spent working in northwest lumber mills. Though he hated the rough and oftentimes vulgar expressions of the mill culture, he knew the experience provided a good balance for him. His work habits and dependability insured that he would have a job every year. One summer he enjoyed a seasonal romance with a girl.

By the time he was a sophomore, Mark met a young man who had been evicted for not paying his rent, and when he couldn't find another apartment, Mark gave him shelter. Dave had a love for art, admired Mark's paintings, and they became friends. Dave told Mark his problems, cried in his arms, and developed an extremely dependent and draining relationship with our son. When Dave was feeling troubled, he would beg Mark, "Come lie down beside me," and Mark would try to comfort him. When Dave made sexual advances, Mark refused. It was not right; Jesus would not be pleased. Dave then found another dependent relationship but continued to live in Mark's apartment for a while.

Dave's new friend, later revealed to be a Satanist masquerading as a Christian, gave him a painting that he hung in their bedroom. It was a picture of a woman's face with white highlights on a black background, a face full of hate, anger, and fear. Dave would go into trances and the face would "speak" to him. Mark was disturbed by this and talked to a Christian woman friend about it. She removed the picture and Dave moved out.

Soon after Mark graduated with a degree in fine arts, he received a call to the ministry and entered seminary. Again, the intensity of the work and study demanded a great deal of energy. Time for fellowship with friends who could refresh him was difficult to find. He found himself persevering in loneliness and functioning on the edge of depression. Fear of homosexual feelings began to rise again. One day at the gym where he went regularly to work out, he met a young man who became his friend. The friendship ended when the fellow wanted to turn a back rub into a sexual experience. "Let's hold each other," he said. Mark needed desperately to be held, but his friend suggested that it would be fun to roll together "like puppies"; though tempted, Mark responded weakly, but with all the strength he could muster, "No." It was wrong.

Mark continued to wrestle with sexual feelings that refused to be put down. Depression lurked more and more as a black pit he frequently fell into. Finally he sought help from a counselor. Hoping to be helped to discover and deal with root causes, he was disappointed to find that the counselor was concerned only with the present. "The past is not relevant. You're not with your parents now. Deal with today's problems." Mark asked for prayer, and the counselor consented, praying along the lines of "God be with you till we meet again." Counseling with this man continued for twelve weeks. It was excellent so far as it went. Mark was helped a great deal. But without the application of forgiveness to cover the past, he was back under the dark cloud of feelings, temptation, and depression three weeks later.

A friend of the family, herself a counselor, came to our home to visit during a holiday time. Mark was home for a visit, fighting his usual battle to resist regressing toward a child's position in the home of his parents. (Everyone struggles in that area until individuation has been accomplished, but it was more of a problem for Mark because, for him, growing up meant facing life-threatening pain alone, then taking on adult roles without having been comforted as a child.) She heard the "Oh, Mark" refrain from the family and mentioned to a friend she didn't like the way he was treated; the friend suggested Mark counsel with her. So, at the age of twenty-five, Mark was called to deal with anger he had begun to allow himself to feel only in the preceding year. First he dealt with his anger toward parents, then his brothers and sisters, then his peers and the world, and finally toward God.

As he recognized and expressed the anger, repented of judgments, and chose to forgive, he fought a fierce battle. As roots that needed inner healing prayer would surface, gay feelings and fears would rise in a huge wave, which then subsided with prayer. Every time a new root surfaced, another wave of attractions arose as well, making it appear as though nothing had been healed. But with each application of prayer for inner healing, the waves subsided to a lower level than before. Again and again the sequence was repeated. At first he could only believe by faith that he was not gay. Finally he *knew* he was not—and declared it!

Satan had a panic attack! Twice while Mark was sleeping he was attacked by an *incubus spirit* (a demonic entity that takes the form of a male and attempts to seduce or rape). Mark took authority over the incubus in the name of the Lord Jesus and commanded it to leave, and it departed. The battle was essentially won. The rest of the story has more to do with claiming and occupying the territory of Mark's life.

Mark no longer felt strong attraction to men. But neither did he feel attracted to girls. He wanted to be married and have children, and he was impatient that God had not yet brought the right woman to him. He was approaching twenty-nine, believing the promise God had given him, "Your wife shall be like a fruitful vine, within your house, your children like olive plants around your table" (Ps. 128:3). But in his heart was the question, "How long, O Lord?" He found himself bemused and bothered by the nagging feeling that girls have ugly bodies. He worked diligently to keep his own muscular body in top shape, wanting nothing in himself to be associated with effeminacy.

Mark came to do his seminary internship in prayer ministry at Elijah House. During that time the Lord brought a young woman named Maureen to visit who was not only lovely inside but also was beautiful enough on the outside to be used effectively by the Lord to gradually overcome that confusing seed and root of "girls have ugly bodies." Mark met her for us at the airport, and the two of them were instantly drawn together. Their courtship proceeded largely by mail and phone calls for a number of months. She came to visit our family again during the summer while Mark was home ministering again with Elijah House. Mark's heart was not healed enough to fully open to anyone, but the Holy Spirit spoke clearly to him that she was "the one," and they were married before he returned to seminary to finish the final quarter necessary for his master of divinity degree. The Lord almost immediately began to reveal what had been so deeply suppressed in Mark's memory and what had kept his heart closed.

The first part of the unveiling is told in our book *Growing Pains* (pages 183–185). Mark had been ministering to two women, and they had been greatly helped. They asked if they could also minister to him, and he consented. The Holy Spirit gave them a word of knowledge in the form of a vision of a little boy standing by a white picket fence near a weeping willow, looking very perplexed. As they shared that picture, the door to Mark's memory was unlocked. He recalled that at the age of five he had gone to spend the afternoon at a farm belonging to some friends of the family. Some teenage boys there ran off beyond a fence into a grove of trees. Mark had been told by us not to go out in back of the house and by the boys not to follow. But he disobeyed and was horrified as he watched them circle around two boys who were engaged in homosexual activity. He tried to hide, but the boys saw him and pursued him. One knocked him down, grabbed him in the groin, violently squeezed, and promised to cut his penis off if he ever told what he had seen. The boys held him, squeezing him and shouting, "Huh, little girl!" "How do you like that, pretty little girl?" "Thought you'd spy on us, didn't you, huh, little girl?" The boys kept talking about all the things they would like to do to that "pretty little girl." That was all that Mark remembered at the time, but he felt relieved as he received prayer ministry concerning the incident. Yet it had been almost like watching a movie of someone else's life; he had felt no emotional response. Several times he said to us, "I think there is more."

Two days later Mark and Maureen quarreled about something, and he found tearfulness greater than the occasion warranted welling up from deep inside. Over the next year at intervals of two to two and a half months, more tears surfaced. Mark and Maureen would see a movie, and unexpectedly the Lord would choose that opportunity to accomplish more healing. In one movie teenagers were making a suicide pact. In another, a child was carried from a burning building by a retarded boy. Another was a story about incest. With each movie, he experienced a profound stirring inside that resulted in his weeping for an hour and a half or more. With each stirring, the Lord enabled him to spontaneously remember additional details of the trauma he had lived so many years before.

A year later Mark dreamed that he shot six men with a machine gun. The six men represented the six teenage boys he had seen at the farm. Two had performed oral sex on each other as the others watched. Recollected pieces of the trauma began to fall into order. When Mark was discovered and caught, several of the boys held him down while *four* forced him to perform oral sex on them. They were so violent he could taste blood in his throat. (The garden hose daydream he had experienced in his fourth-grade classroom was caused by this memory trying to rise to consciousness.) Not only did they promise to cut off his penis if he told anyone, but they also told him they would kill his parents. That, he said, was the most fearful threat of all. He could not tell anyone. He walked under an unbearable weight of guilt! He felt under conviction that because he had disobeyed in going behind the house, this horrible thing had come about. He was convinced that if he disobeyed again, something worse was sure to happen. He made an inner vow not to let his masculinity show, if this was what it was to be masculine, and totally suppressed memory of the incident. Only a few days after the trauma, he caught a glimpse of several of the boys on the street in town and was terribly afraid. But he didn't know why.

The Lord had compassion on His wounded child and took initiative to set him free. Jesus said in John 10:10–11:

> The thief comes only to steal, and kill, and destroy; I came that they might have life, and might have it abundantly. I am the good shepherd; the good shepherd lays down His life for the sheep.

No one knew what Mark's trouble was, but Jesus promised:

> For nothing is hidden that shall not become evident, nor anything secret that shall not be known and come to light.
> —LUKE 8:17

As the Holy Spirit revealed the root sources of wounding, Mark made choices to forgive, and the Lord empowered those choices and gave them reality. Mark fought a good fight to choose what was pleasing to the Lord, and the Lord brought people to minister to him. "The LORD is for me among those who help me; therefore I shall look with satisfaction on those who hate me" (Ps. 118:7).

He persevered despite anxiety attacks. In one letter, he shared:

> The most prominent roots of anxiety were these: a fear of disapproval, because I needed Dad's approval; and a fear of success because I did not want to be stamped into Dad's mold by becoming like him. Dad had little fault in this latter matter (except perhaps with the "army" episode). He had always been good about not pressing me into the ministry. But in my heart I reacted vehemently to anyone getting control over my identity and me (as those boys did, who tried to cast me in the mold of "pretty little girl"). So I was especially alert to little sleights that hit an old bruise—and people asking me if I was going to "follow in (my) father's footsteps."

During the healing process, Mark was attacked in his sleep many times by demonic powers trying to suffocate him. During waking hours and with the help of others, Mark experienced the power of the name of Jesus as he exercised *authority* in the risen Lord to cast away demons (representing such things as hate, anger, murder, and desire for anonymity) that had taken opportunity to harass and oppress him because he had held those attitudes in his heart. He took *authority* in Jesus to break his own inner vow to hide masculinity and was set free to grow into the fullness of what God created him to be. As the Lord has made known each aspect of hurts and his responses to hurts, Mark and Maureen have prayed about them, bringing their effects to death on the cross of Jesus.

One night Mark dreamed a vivid and significant dream describing blessed victory. Mark was in a big white house with pretty wooden floors (the appearance of the parsonage in which we lived when he was five). In the dream we had left him to care for the parsonage for a few weeks, and he had decided to take pride in it like it was his own. He turned the heat up because it was cold and cleaned and ordered it from top to bottom. Then he looked up to see a woman coming down the stairs. She said to him, "I used to own this place, but now that you've cleaned it so well, I have to leave." With that, she left.

As Mark related the whole of his story to me, I could have wept bitterly for the boy had I not been so intensely proud of the *man*—and so overwhelmingly grateful to the Lord for His faithfulness to deliver, heal, restore, and bless so as to transform a devastated five-year-old into a healer of today's wounded.

I know that there are countless numbers of molested boys and girls who have grown to adulthood without ever having left the shatteredness and confusion of their childhood behind. It is never too late to receive healing and transformation. A word from the Word to the wounded: God knows and cares about you. And, with your invitation, He is able to save forever those who draw near to God through Him (Jesus Christ), since He always lives to make intercession for them (Heb. 7:25).

> It is not the will of your Father who is in heaven that one of these little ones perish.
>
> —MATTHEW 18:14

Chapter 3

SUPPRESSION, REGRESSION, AND FRIGIDITY

But this is a people plundered and despoiled; all of them are trapped in caves, or are hidden away in prisons; they have become a prey with none to deliver them, and a spoil, with none to say, "Give them back!" Who among you will give ear to this? Who will give heed and listen hereafter?

ISAIAH 42:22–23

INNER VOWS

I HAVE DESCRIBED THE FEMALE ABUSE VICTIM AS ONE WHO RUNS, commonly into promiscuity. We have ministered to some whose promiscuity led to a period in their lives when they were in bondage also to prostitution, particularly where alcohol and/or drugs have laid hold. In many, however, there is a flight response that takes them in the opposite direction from promiscuity. A girl may react to sexual abuse in a way that causes her to make a deep inner vow, which, if verbalized, would sound something like the following: "I will *never* again let myself get into a position where what begins as something clean and wholesome [simply needing to be loved and affirmed] can become nasty, abhorrent, and destructive."

This kind of vow may be conscious or unconscious. It may be

completely forgotten as the years go on. But it is registered in the inner person as a powerfully controlling and blocking directive, resulting in sexual dysfunction. On the surface, a woman may want very much to be intimate and uninhibited with her husband, but she finds herself in bondage to an automatic defensive turn-off mechanism each time he approaches her. She *cannot* really meet him, and even though for his sake or to protect the marriage she may choose to go through the motions of intercourse, she is unable to experience sexual pleasure, let alone climax. It is not uncommon for such women to complain of vaginal discomfort. At best, sexual intercourse becomes a duty and a chore they will avoid whenever possible.

FRIGIDITY

Many times we have been called to minister to such women who have no conscious memory of having been molested. *Frigidity* can be the result of other sorts of wounding as well, or a result of transmission of unhealthy attitudes, physical impairment, or of inadequate training. Nevertheless, when we as prayer ministers explore possible causes for frigidity, we routinely consider the possibility of suppressed memories of abuse.

From experience we have learned what we have known by faith—that the Lord is a perfect gentleman. He *will* "bring to light the things hidden in the darkness" (1 Cor. 4:5). But we are told in the first part of that text that we are to "*wait* until the *Lord* comes." He will never stir something to rise from our inner being unless He knows that we have been prepared to deal with it. Neither will He violate our free will.

It is for these reasons that we have strongly opposed the use of hypnotism to reveal what is hidden in the unconscious. Although Scripture does not mention hypnotism by name (the word *hypnotism* was not invented until the 1800s), we find it is disturbingly similar to spell casting, which is forbidden in Deuteronomy 18:11. The Hebrew word there for "spell" is *chabar*, which means, "to fascinate—charm."[1] We also believe that hypnotism is incompatible with the nature of Christ, for it is no gentleman. It will sometimes stir things to rise from the unconscious before the person is ready to face them and be healed.

As we minister, sometimes the Holy Spirit will show us a repressed memory of molestation. In such cases, we do not reveal it to the person to whom we are ministering, for that would steal from her the enterprise of discovery (not to mention open us up to a charge of "false memory"). Rather, we write down the revelation and continue to deal with other issues until she remembers on her own. Then we show her what we wrote down as a confirmation.

When we pray about the memory, we celebrate God's love for the person, inviting Jesus to communicate love to her in her environment, being where she has remained a wounded child. The following are sample prayers, not to be used as formulas:

> *Thank You, Lord, that You love this woman and have longed to set her free. You grieved for her when she was molested, and You have carried her pain and sorrow in Your heart all these years. We invite You now, Lord, to go to the depths of her heart where the little girl has felt so afraid, so unclean, so used, and ashamed. Pour in Your perfect love to cast out all her fear. Speak to her heart and let her know that You accept her and love her just as she is, and that there is no way she can lose that love. Draw all of her pain and shame to Yourself, Lord, and fill her wounds with healing balm. (See Isaiah 53:4.)*

To enable her (as an adult and as her inner child) to forgive the man who violated her, we might pray:

> *Lord, we ask You to enable the heart of the little girl inside to forgive.*

Then we may ask, "Can you put it in your own words that you are willing to forgive? All God asks you to do is to choose. He is the one who accomplishes it and makes it real."

The woman may respond, "Yes. Lord, I choose to forgive. And I ask forgiveness for closing my heart and hurting my husband and others who love me."

After that, we pray to give assurance of forgiveness:

Thank You, Lord, that Your Word is true and Your forgiveness is sure (Matt. 6:14; 1 John 1:9). You are forgiven in the name of our Lord Jesus Christ, according to His promises (John 20:23). Jesus, lift away her sense of unworthiness.

We pray to invite cleansing:

Lord Jesus, thank You that You are washing her clean right now. Let the rivers of Your living water flow over and through her, carrying away all the filth of defilement. Continue to pour Your cleansing streams into her until she feels squeaky clean and refreshed.

We ask the Lord to separate her spirit from that of the molester (see chapter 4):

Bring Your sword of truth, Lord, and separate her spirit from the man who molested her. In the authority of Jesus, we direct her spirit to forget the union. By Your grace and power, Lord, let her memory of that experience be so transformed that it can no longer afflict her or hold her in bondage. Let it become, instead, a part of her wisdom and compassion.

We pray to bring habit structures to death on the cross, break her inner vows, and loose her to come to life in freedom:

We ask You, Lord, to bring to death on the cross the habits she practiced in relating to her husband. By the authority of Jesus we break the power of her inner vow not to be vulnerable. Melt her heart. Give her a new and right spirit. We loose her in the power of the living Lord to be free to bless her husband and to come to the fullness of what You intended her to be. Enable her, Lord, to walk in all that You have accomplished. Thank You.

Such a woman's life is now a testimony of what St. Paul was talking about when he spoke of "forgetting what lies behind and reaching forward to what lies ahead" (Phil. 3:13). Forgetting is never accomplished by ignoring memories or by suppressing them. Hurts and resultant practices never truly "lie behind" us until they find their effective death on the cross. Conversion begins to apply the cross. Counseling and prayer complete the work of redemption begun at conversion. Suppression of hurtful memories creates a pile of painful baggage, weighing us down with unseen "burdens hard to bear" (Luke 11:46). They prevent us from functioning freely. If pressured by subsequent traumas, disappointments, and hurts, they become volcanoes that eventually gather enough driving force to cause explosions. It is from the "treasure" of our hearts that we express good and evil (Luke 6:45). "But all things become visible when they are exposed by the light, for *everything that becomes visible is light*" (Eph. 5:13, emphasis added).

It is only as we allow the Lord to expose our hearts' "treasures" to the light of His grace, compassion, and forgiveness that we can apply the cross to our practiced responses and effectively reckon them as dead (Rom. 6:10–14).

As we who minister do so in His grace, expressing His sensitive compassion even in the midst of stern confrontation, we communicate the nature of the Lord's love. Jesus becomes flesh through us, and the wounded one is enabled gradually to open to trust our love and therefore His. Sexually abused people have been so fractured in ability to trust authority that their minds say they believe the Lord and want Him to help them, but often their spirits recoil in fear and distrust.

Therefore they need "love with skin on." They require gentle, persistent human "wooing" until experience enables the heart to allow the Lord to heal.

Repression of Painful Memories

Repressed sexual abuse may surface in many ways. Carrie was a gifted leader of a prayer group in her church. She had come to know the Lord through a great deal of suffering in her own life and had been forgiven much. The Lord's transforming power had comforted many waste places in her heart and had changed many of her personal deserts into gardens (Isa. 51:3) so that she could identify with the needs of others and minister with humility and compassion.

The Holy Spirit equipped her with gifts of insight into the hidden motivations of people. "The purposes of a man's heart are deep waters, but a man of understanding draws them out" (Prov. 20:5, NIV). As she and her group ministered to one another, Carrie found herself experiencing what she at first identified as burden-bearing identification with others who had been sexually abused as children. Then she began to realize that some of the brief images coming to her were bits and pieces from her own memory stream!

In her dreams and daydreams, Carrie often appeared as the victim. When she began to suspect that her own father had abused her, she strongly resisted the possibility. She had loved him so dearly! How could he have betrayed her love and trust? But the snatches of memory persisted, and she began to feel physically ill whenever the subject arose.

When she recognized and finally accepted that the Holy Spirit was bringing to light memories she had suppressed for years, she sought healing. The Lord did not cause her to relive the past in full detail. He brought to consciousness only enough to make her aware of her need, and forgiveness and healing were accomplished on the basis of faith. Some have erred as prayer ministers by making a technique of trying to cause people to relive childhood experiences. For the sexually abused, that can be especially excruciating—and unnecessary. The Lord sometimes chooses to allow a person to relive a memory or a portion of a memory, but we should not make this a formula. We received salvation by faith. Healing can be received the same way.

Jean struggled with a variety of problems—her intense need to be needed, fear of rejection, an inability to be truly corporate (to relate in unity, to be "one" with another). Unmarried, she repeatedly wormed her way into the middle of husband-and-wife relationships, not to engage in any sort of affair, but to find refuge there with a degree of inordinate demand that she could not acknowledge. Outsiders saw her as a very loving and generous person, which indeed she was. People who knew her well and loved her sought to minister to the roots of her insecurities, particularly in regard to her obesity, which eroded her self-esteem.

Healing was accomplished to a degree in some areas, but she persisted in denial of her weight problem. "I've always been this way. I don't have an eating disorder." The Holy Spirit revealed to her what she had suppressed—sexual molestation by a family member when she was little more than an infant. Her ability to trust had been destroyed from the beginning. She had never again learned to open her heart to be met and nurtured. Eating had become both a substitute for love and comfort, and a way of hiding her beauty from whoever might be attracted and tempted to dishonor and hurt her. She had built obesity as her shield to protect a wounded, fearful child. The grown woman knew intellectually that God is her sure defense. But her childish heart could not believe it. Her attempting to cuddle between husbands and wives was nothing more than a little child within the grown adult, trying to recapture and bask in the security between her parents that had been fractured by the molestation.

FANTASIZING

Another flight mechanism we have seen is the practice of *fantasizing*. If a victim of sexual abuse is unable to avoid repeated violation and is too fearful to seek help, she may learn to cope by pretending that she is someone else or somewhere else. She turns off her feelings and either focuses her thoughts far away or goes into mental and emotional limbo as her abuser uses her body as a "thing"—from which she has temporarily detached. This defensive practice often becomes habitual in such a person so as to render her incapable of experiencing full union with her husband in sex years later, even though intellectually she may think she has resolved these issues.

Tina was such a person. When we met her, she had been married for ten years to a man who loved her with consistent gentleness and respect. He worked steadily and provided well for his wife and their two daughters. He was emotionally stable and attentive to their needs, often at his own expense. Tina counted herself blessed to be married to such a man and did all she could to keep a neat home, cook wholesome meals, and take an interest in the things that were important to him. But she could not fully give herself sexually to him.

Involuntarily she tensed when he so much as touched her. By a sheer act of her will she chose to let him make love to her, but compulsively she would flee immediately into a fantasy world and stay there until he had satisfied himself. He was sensitive enough to know that she was not present with him, and he struggled with rejection, anger, and loneliness until finally, to protect his own sensitivities, he found himself withdrawing from her as much as possible. Tina knew her guilt in the matter and sought prayer ministry.

She revealed that from the time she was eight, she had been sexually abused by her father and some of his drinking friends, and then by her brothers and boy cousins. At first she was only teased, with suggestive comments and crude jokes, then by touching that soon proceeded to fondling and culminated in repeated experiences of incest. She had been defiled, undefended, trapped, and had endured obscenities in the only way she knew how—by escaping through her imagination.

The abuse continued until she reached the age of sixteen and left home to marry her husband. Though she wasn't sure she loved him (certainly not romantically), he was the first man who had ever treated her like a lady. He told her she was beautiful and special, the most wonderful thing that had happened to him.

Prior to this, she had always felt used, dirty, and ugly, good for nothing but sexual games. This prince of a man never approached her in any way that even hinted of disrespect. Because of his consistent, considerate treatment of her, because he patiently gave her all the space she needed during their courtship, and because he fulfilled every promise he made, she dared to trust him enough to vow to be his wife.

In her mind she said, "With him it will be different. There is nothing to fear in him." But the habits built into the computer of her heart commanded, "Turn off. Play it safe. You're vulnerable now. You could be hurt." Once or twice when the guilt for the pain she was inflicting on her husband overtook her, she struggled fiercely to countermand the fear in her heart and began to open. But old memories flooded up so powerfully she fled into oblivion again.

Tina's telling of her story was interspersed with weeping and exclamations of hopelessness and self-condemnation:

"I can't make myself act differently! I don't know why my husband puts up with me! I know I'm going to lose him. I'm such a mess! Maybe I've always been bad! If something hadn't been wrong with me, maybe those awful things wouldn't have happened to me!"

"No, Tina," we responded. "You're not a bad person. You're a beautiful child of God, and you've been severely wounded by some very sick people. We're amazed that you've done so well!"

"I ain't done nuthin' right!"

"We know the Lord is proud of you for trying. And He wants to comfort and heal you and make something beautiful out of your life."

"He didn't seem too anxious to do nuthin' about that when I was a kid."

"We can surely see how you'd feel that way. Can you understand that God won't force anybody to be kind and loving? He leaves us all free to make our choices. When parents get all mixed up and injure the children He gave them to love, Father God grieves."

"I should hope!"

"He's ready and able to heal your wounds and set you free to enjoy the rest of your life, if you'll let Him."

"So, what if I ask Him and nuthin' happens?"

"So, what have you got to lose? Let's give Him a chance. We believe He's been waiting a long time for this moment."

She gave a short sigh, shrugged her shoulders, and closed her eyes. "OK," she said. "We'll see."

We proceeded to minister to her, through prayer, inviting the Lord to pour His presence with healing power into the depths of the woundedness in her spirit. It was not enough to pray only for the adult Tina. Knowing that she was still trapped in her childhood emotions, we asked Jesus to transcend time and minister to the eight-year-old who was still living deep inside her grown-up body. (If Jesus does not transcend time, we might as well forget the cross—it was done two thousand years ago! Praise God He is not limited to our faulty concepts of time; He can reach and touch any point in our lives, from conception to the present.)

> When I was a child, I used to speak as a child, think as a child, reason as a child; when I became a man, I did away with childish things. For now we see in a mirror dimly, but then face to face; now I know in part, but then I shall know fully just as I also have been fully known.
>
> —1 CORINTHIANS 13:11–12

As the Lord ministered to the wound deep down in Tina's heart, she received comfort, healing, and the holy gift of a seed of trust. As prayers of affirmation were repeated again and again, the eyes of her heart were enlightened to know the hope of the Lord's calling her to an inheritance in Him (Eph. 1:18). Her spirit was given strength then to forgive and to begin to do away with the childish thoughts and reasoning that had blinded and imprisoned her. She chose life.

CHOOSING LIFE

Choosing life and being *able* to walk in it are not one and the same. Tina had to learn what clean, healthy parenting is by experiencing it. Her husband was not the one to reparent her. A husband who tries to fill father vacancies in his wife may only further complicate her role confusion. Wives don't make love to fathers. Her counselors did not have the time to provide the reparenting. But an older couple in their church took her under their wing for a while, carrying her in their hearts (Phil. 1:7) and interceding for her. She was welcomed and encouraged to visit in their home as a beloved daughter. They listened to her, talked with her, prayed with her, and affirmed her again and again, teaching her to know who she is in Christ. They did as St. Paul did:

> For if you were to have countless tutors in Christ, yet you would not have many fathers; for in Christ Jesus I became father through the gospel. I exhort you therefore, be imitators of me.
> —1 CORINTHIANS 4:15–16

The older couple did not treat Tina as a child, nor did they allow her to relate to them as a small child would. They were as affectionate with her as she allowed them to be. If she had a decision to make, they did not offer advice in a directive or controlling manner. That would have made her dependent upon them and would have taken from her the enterprise of her life. Rather, they offered to help her understand the advantages and disadvantages of possible alternatives and prayed with her that she might be able to choose wisely. When she made mistakes, they encouraged her to think through and verbalize what she had learned. They endured her emotional outbursts without taking anything personally, and when she had vented her feelings, they would ask, "Tina, who are you *really* upset at?" As she learned to identify her feelings and they prayed together, Tina was introduced to a Father God with whom she could relate openly and honestly without fear of condemnation or harm.

Sometimes Tina would do something deliberately ornery to test her parents-in-the-Lord. Occasionally she was too demanding of their time and attention. She learned from their responses what it means to be confronted in love. As the relationship continued, the Lord Himself nurtured areas of Tina's heart that held wounds from her childhood that had never been fed or taught, or held accountable in healthy, appropriate ways. As Tina observed a mother and father in Christ relating wholesomely to one another, she became an imitator of them. As she experienced their unconditional love and clean affection toward her, she was set free to choose to grow into the fullness of what the Lord had created her to be. And prayers were said to bring her genealogical inheritance to a stopping place on the cross of Christ.

Since that time she has been growing day by day into her inheritance as a mature child of God. Her parents in Christ have now become her friends who coach, encourage, reprove, and exhort her as she exercises a daily discipline of reckoning herself dead to the ways of the past, calling upon the Lord moment by moment to empower new choices. As with all of us, her growth has not been a steady, upward journey. It could be described more accurately by what sociologists have called "dip-surge-plateau-dip-surge…" But her dips are becoming much less severe, her surges increasingly empowered, and her plateaus more enduring and peaceful.

REGRESSION

Regression is another escape pattern we have observed in those who have been sexually abused. One of the most dramatic examples in our counseling experience was Margie. She had spent several periods of her young adult life, following suicide attempts, in psychiatric hospitals. She had struggled unsuccessfully with anorexia/bulimia. When her friends called to make an appointment for her, these facts of her history were not communicated to us.

We are accustomed to having people come from distant places to spend a number of days in intense prayer ministry with those who facilitate prayer ministry at Elijah House. Since we do not have a facility to house clients, and hospitality in private homes is not always available, most have found comfortable and inexpensive lodging in nearby motels.

Margie arrived alone, having driven over six hundred miles. The seriousness of her condition did not manifest itself during the initial interview with one of our staff. During the next sessions, however, in the midst of prayer Margie suddenly regressed to a child of two. This happened as the prayer minister prayed, but it was not initiated by the one who ministered to her. We are aware that some who minister in the area of healing employ techniques that are designed to cause people to recall childhood traumas experientially. This has never been our practice, nor has it been the way of those trained by us. Margie's prayer minister simply prayed that the Lord would take charge of all that they had discussed that day and that He would begin to heal her innermost being and enable her to make choices to forgive those who had wounded her from the time she was a very little girl. Her regression was spontaneous—and it lasted for three days! A Christian family consented to receive her into their home (with fear and trembling), and they tenderly cared for her as she toddled with her thumb in her mouth, dragging a small blanket behind her. Her infrequent speech was baby talk. She played with her food. Quite often she would be found hiding in a closet and had to be coaxed out with assurances of protection. After those three days of patient encouragement, undergirded by intercessory prayer, the grown woman reemerged, and ministry continued with the prayer minister.

Bit by bit, Margie was able to share memories of gross sexual abuse by her father, sexual violation from boys she dated, and finally molestation by a clergyman to whom she went for help.

Difficulties in interpersonal relationships frequently result from poor resolution of [the normal] conflict between the trust necessary for intimacy and the mistrust necessary for self-protection. Women who were sexually abused as children may be inordinately wary of the most devoted lover, or naïvely trusting of the most exploitive lover. Many of these women have a history of repeated abusive relationships with men. Some studies have also reported an increased risk of rape in adulthood among women who were victims of incest in childhood, perhaps reflecting diminished self-protective functions....

Many communities offer self-help or specialized therapy groups for victims of sexual trauma. Appropriate resources often include rape crisis centers, women's centers, shelters for abused women, and therapists who have taken a particular interest in this area. Selection of a therapist must be done cautiously. Various surveys have revealed up to 10 percent of therapists acknowledge becoming sexually involved with their patients. Such a lack of therapeutic boundaries, coupled with a patient who may sexualize needs for approval and affection, may lead to destructive [repetition] of the trauma.[2]

Each time the Lord began to stir an unconfessed recollection, Margie would regress again for hours or days until patient love and gentle confrontation, undergirded by prayer, strengthened, invited, and encouraged her to share. Each memory she related, along with every response, was taken to the cross in prayer. Over a period of a year we joyfully witnessed the Lord's transformation of her life.

She learned from her host family and people in the church what wholesome relationships are. She experienced clean affection and learned to discern and welcome trustworthy hugs. The teenage son of her host family was an almost constant initiator of therapeutic laughter with his ridiculous but respectful banter and teasing. Margie related to him as if she were in her teens, although she was thirty. Her medical problems were treated by a physician, and her diet was supervised. She became a contributing member of the household, delighting in the care of the garden and helping in the kitchen. Her mind was renewed as she attended local Christian education classes and seminars on inner healing and Christian family life. She participated in a home fellowship group in the church and learned to minister to others.

As the time for her return to her home city approached, she suddenly regressed once more. Her parents-in-Christ called us for help: "What are we going to do?" We prayed, and the Lord indicated clearly that now it was time for simple confrontation. John found her under her bed, with her thumb in her mouth. He lifted the bedspread and said to her, "This is enough, young lady! You are no longer regressing. You are *choosing* to act like a child, and you are *not* going to treat those who have loved you to life this way! If you aren't upstairs within the hour helping to can those beans, we're shipping you home tomorrow!" He turned and left the room. In less than a half hour Margie appeared in the kitchen, asking, "What can I do to help?"

In the next ministry session, one more dramatically devastating memory of her father rose to the surface to be forgiven and released to the Lord. Margie chose to return to her native city a short time later. Many months after that, Margie discovered that the childhood abuse was far more extensive than we knew, and that what Margie had experienced under the bed was what is called an abreaction—the reliving of the terror of some past memory not yet discovered. At that moment, it was as if Margie literally was three years old again, incapable of responding as an adult. If John had known that, he would have approached her far more tenderly, not expecting her to snap out of it so quickly. But God still came through, though our knowledge at the time was partial.

Before she left, Margie testified in church that for the first time in her life she was no longer preoccupied with thoughts of death. She had chosen life and was full of gratitude to God and His people for setting her free from the part of her past that was visible at the time and for nurturing her with love so she could begin to trust again to take hold of the blessings of life God has available for her. Later, under someone else's care, she continued to deal with past traumas until she found more complete healing.

"For you were formerly darkness, but now you are light in the Lord; walk as children of light" (Eph. 5:8). Margie's family in the Lord continued to correspond with her and uphold her in prayer as she walked on her new feet. She later worked full-time and maintained her own apartment. She invested her life as part of a small group within her church and grew in the Lord as she participated in a street ministry to alcoholics and drug addicts.

Chapter 4

A GARLAND FOR ASHES— THE HEALING PROCESS

The Spirit of the Lord GOD is upon me, because the LORD has anointed me to bring good news to the afflicted; He has sent me to build up the brokenhearted, to proclaim liberty to captives, and freedom to prisoners....To comfort all who mourn...giving them a garland instead of ashes, the oil of gladness instead of mourning, the mantle of praise instead of a spirit of fainting. So they will be called oaks of righteousness, the planting of the LORD, that He may be glorified.

ISAIAH 61:1–3

THE GOOD NEWS OF THE LORD'S POWER AND INTENT IS "TO SET free those who are downtrodden" (Luke 4:18). Perhaps no one is more downtrodden and brokenhearted than the sexually abused. The father of the prodigal son rejoiced that his son who "was dead...has come to life again" (Luke 15:24), but the prodigal son's death was due to his own sins. The sexually abused are just as dead due to the sins of others. When the Lord summons the sexually abused to life again, pastors, counselors, relatives, and friends who love them are called to respond to the command of Jesus to, "Unbind him, and let him go" (John 11:44).

Years ago my husband, John, played the part of Lazarus in a drama in a family camp. When the one who played Jesus called out, "Lazarus, come forth," John found that his own heart had moved beyond the drama into reality! He felt the "comfort" of death. Whatever Lazarus may have felt when Jesus called, John did not want to come back to life. The risks and hurts of life hardly seemed worth comparing to the prospect of escape to heaven. But John has had a relatively happy life and has never been torn by molestation or abuse. Consider how reluctant, how hesitant, and how fearful a sexually abused person may feel when Jesus calls him/her to life!

This means that whether we are His "royal priesthood" (1 Pet. 2:9) as prayer ministers or as relatives and friends, we need to understand clearly the need for sensitivity and patient perseverance. We must be careful not to hurry the abused, both in bringing to the cross their sinful responses and in restoring them to happy life.

Healing of the heart requires time for anyone, but much more for the abused. Rushing in too soon with unenlightened, fleshly zeal can rape the process of healing and inflict new wounds on already tortured hearts. The trust levels of those who have been sexually abused have been so fractured that it is a painful and fearful thing for them to be ready and willing to receive the holy gift of new life in Jesus.

We must beware of callous programs that disrespect the tenderness of the sexually wounded. Whenever John and I teach about inner healing and transformation, we attempt to discourage reliance upon techniques and methods, though wisdom certainly instructs us to learn from the ways others do things. We encourage gathering as much knowledge and skill as possible to stock our ministry shelves. We are then equipped with a rich supply of ingredients for healing. If we can remain humble, divested of gimmicks and of reliance upon our own fleshly knowledge, the Holy Spirit can then direct us as He deems appropriate. This, of course, implies necessity to abide in the presence of the Lord and to be growing daily in skills of listening and gifts of discernment.

The following *ingredients* are *not* to be followed "1-2-3" as though they were a formula for ministering to the sexually abused, but rather as a guide to what needs to be done at the right times in the process of healing.

INTERCESSORY PRAYER FOR THE CONDITION OF THE INNER MAN

Intercessory prayer is the most powerful foundational tool we have. By it we invite the Lord *to accomplish the work He has already initiated.*

> The LORD longs to be gracious to you, and therefore He waits on high to have compassion on you. For the LORD is a God of justice; how blessed are all those who long for Him.
> —ISAIAH 30:18

By intercessory prayer we *prepare* the heart of the wounded one so that he is enabled to receive healing and blessing.

> I pray that *the eyes of your heart may be enlightened*, so that you may know what is the hope of His calling, what are the riches of the glory of His inheritance in the saints, and what is the surpassing greatness of His power toward us who believe.
> —EPHESIANS 1:18–19,
> emphasis added

A child or adult who has hardened and closed her heart in order not to be vulnerable needs strength in her "inner man" (personal spirit) by the gift of the Holy Spirit in order to have the capacity to come to life. In prayer we ask the Lord to pour in His gift of strength, to melt the heart of stone with His love (Ezek. 36:26), and to shine His light into the darkened eyes of the heart.

INTERCESSORY PRAYER FOR
PROTECTION AND RESTORATION

Recognizing that the one for whom we pray has closed her heart to God because of her loss of trust in authority figures, and by this has made herself vulnerable to the power of darkness, we need also to stand in the gap interceding for her protection.

One time we were carrying Susie, a young teenager, in intercessory burden. Her father had violated her repeatedly for a period of several years. So far as we knew, the molestation had not progressed beyond fondling. However, studies show that over a period of time fondling is just as emotionally damaging as full incest. Susie's reactions certainly supported that contention. Overwhelmed by hurt, anger, and fear, she fled into irrational running. When her father was removed from the home and the actual threat of molestation was no longer present, she continued to emotionally identify home with vulnerability to hurt. For her, whatever damage might lurk in the world away from home loomed only as an unknown theoretical enemy. She had been overcome, used, and bruised by the enemy she had known *at home*.

When her father left, and enough time and ministry to establish a peaceful nurturing home environment had been given to the family, everyone expected Susie to settle down and rest. But at the height of "everything is becoming so good!" she suddenly disappeared with no explanation, which was devastatingly mind-boggling to her mother. The police were notified to be watching for her. Nearly two weeks went by with no word from Susie. Her family and friends continually interceded for her: "Lord, let Your presence go with her. If she makes her 'bed in Sheol' or dwells in the 'remotest part of the sea,' let 'Thy right hand lay hold of [her]' (Ps. 139:8–10). If need be, Lord, grab her up by the scruff of the neck! Send Your holy angels to accompany her wherever she is. In the name of Jesus we command the powers of darkness to stand back from her. Lord, lift the dark clouds of confusion from her. Let Your light shine upon her. Let her be saturated with Your love, and let Your strength fill her spirit. Put Your shield about her. Cleave through her with Your sword of truth, and restore her to You and her family and to her rightful mind. Thank You, Lord."

One day the family received a report that Susie had been in an automobile accident and was being treated for bruises and cuts in a hospital emergency room. Her mother hastened to pick her up, but she and her "friends"—with whom she had been riding around, living out of a car—fled before her mother could get there.

Once again it was down-on-the-knees intercessory time for family and friends! "Lord, we know You are faithful. Though Susie is denying You and all who truly care about her right now, we know that she is never lost for a moment from Your sight or from Your love. Pursue her. Bring to death on Your cross the identification she has made between home and danger. Remind her of warm mother hugs, good times with brothers and grandparents, favorite foods, and times of laughter around the table. Put Your cross between her and the influence of those who feed her confusion with their own rebellion, anger, hatred, and fear. In Your wisdom, Lord, use whatever misery and pain she is experiencing to bring her to the end of her delusions. Speak Your love and ours to her spirit, Lord. Give her no peace till she returns."

Susie returned—and left—and returned again—and then received *extensive* ministry from some of the *best* prayer ministers in America. Intercessory prayer continually undergirded the counseling. "Let Your wisdom, love, and healing power express to her through them, Lord. Let the enemy be scattered! Give her new roots in You. Root and ground her in love." She came home having dedicated her life to Jesus, making positive declarations of what she planned to do with her life. Relatives and friends cried out, "Hallelujah, Lord, she's going to make it!"

But when Susie was required to repeat a grade because of truancy, awkwardness developed in her relationships at school, and her high IQ made her classes seem boring. Loneliness then made her easy prey for misguided advice and comfort from the local dropout population. By the end of only one week she was off and running again! This time she went with a boyfriend with whom she had developed a deeply dependent relationship.

As family and friends sought the Lord for direction regarding how to pray, He said clearly, "Break the unholy bonds." They prayed persistently, in those words. They continued to ask that love, strength, and truth be poured into Susie, that she would be enabled to know herself and to stand and make decisions as the person God created her to be, free from confusion and persuasion from her peers. They prayed that the Lord would somehow break the tyranny of emotion that held her in bondage to the feelings of the moment and restore her ability to weigh consequences with a true conscience.

CONFRONTATION AND RELEASE OF THE LORD'S DISCIPLINE

Once more Susie was brought home by the police. This time her irate defiance was met by *stern* confrontation from her family. "Young lady, we care about you much more than you care about yourself. Nothing you can do will make us stop loving you. But you have trashed everything that anyone has done to try to help you! We understand your feelings, but we have feelings too! We have lain awake night after night agonizing over where you might be, knowing full well what happens to hundreds of kids on the street! You can choose to throw away the rest of your life if you want to. We don't know what else to do. We're releasing you now to the discipline of the Lord." "*He* disciplines us *for our good*" (Heb. 12:10, emphasis added).

The Lord then directed her family to give her a scripture to read that described the results of rejecting the Lord's discipline.

> ...because they hated knowledge, and did not choose the fear of the LORD. They would not accept my counsel, they spurned all my reproof. So they shall eat the fruit of their own way, and be satiated with their own devices. For the waywardness of the naïve shall kill them, and the complacency of fools shall

destroy them. But he who listens to me shall live securely, and shall be at ease from the dread of evil.

—Proverbs 1:29–33

In the middle of the night Susie ran away again. This time she was gone for only three days. When she returned, she apologized for her behavior and announced, " I'm home. I'm going to see if I can get back into school, and it's *my choice!*" the following two months proved to be a time of reconciliation and rebonding with her mother and brothers.

Susie's family and friends don't yet know the ending of the story; years later she is still in a growing process, but they know the Lord. They know that if they have to endure another round of running, they will "*not fear evil tidings*" for their "heart is steadfast, *trusting in the LORD*" (Ps. 112:7, emphasis added). Evil tidings are temporary. God is eternally faithful.

They believe concerning Susie, "I am confident of this very thing, that *He who began a good work in you will perfect it* until the day of Christ Jesus" (Phil. 1:6, emphasis added). Meanwhile, intercession on her behalf, along with affirmative expressions of appreciation and unconditional loving affection, supplies her with supportive strength.

Let the reader note that prayers for Susie were never either controlling or manipulating. The Lord, who was paying the price not to deprive her of free will, would not hear manipulative petitions. Rather, the intercessions of family and friends were designed to deliver her from that which would imprison and prevent her from being her own person. They were prayers to restore her free will from captivity and to equip her to make her own choices.

Intercession never guarantees success, because the Lord never forces anyone to accept His good gifts. Intercession plants the cross of Christ between a person's sowing and reaping, keeps the door open to God, and blocks the devil's interference. Effective intercessors must never take personally any attacks, rejections, or seeming failures except to inquire of God how they might respond more obediently within His will and His nature.

FORGIVENESS GIVEN

The Word of God never gives anyone nice options about forgiving. Jesus clearly stated, "For if you forgive men for their transgressions, your heavenly Father will also forgive you. But if you do not forgive men, then your Father will not forgive your transgressions" (Matt. 6:14–15). We are not allowed loopholes by which to consider ourselves exceptions by virtue of the horrendous nature of crimes against us. God knows that harbored bitterness brews deadly poisons within; poisons have the capacity to destroy us and defile those around us. For that reason Hebrews 12:14–15 (emphasis added) gives us this command:

> *Pursue* peace with all men, and the sanctification without which no one will see the Lord. *See to it* that no one comes short of the grace of God; that no root of bitterness springing up causes trouble, and by it many be defiled.

Since we see, hear, and speak from that which fills our hearts (Luke 6:45), unforgiveness, hatred, and bitterness lodged in the treasure chests of our hearts pervert all perceptions and adversely affect all our relationships.

Until they forgive, the sexually abused can never find freedom. However, we must not rush to minister this truth, wielding God's law as a club. There is a time for everything, and "He has made everything appropriate in its time" (Eccles. 3:11).

Wounded people need to let feelings live and to express them—not indiscriminately to wound others—but to confess them honestly to God and to those who counsel and minister.

Catharsis (verbal expression of feelings for the purpose of relieving tension and anxiety) is cleansing and healthy—until it becomes mere rehearsal. Those who minister need to communicate unconditional love and acceptance as they encourage the cleansing ventilation of cathartic confessions. Then when they perceive that continued verbalizing of negative feelings is only serving to entrench the people to whom they minister farther into the tyranny of their feelings, prayer ministers must confrontationally "[speak] the truth in love" (Eph. 4:15). The need to pray for the enabling of right choices in the person becomes the prayer minister's responsibility also. Having taken time to listen, prayer ministers would do well at this point to become sensitively bold to make the people they minister to aware of their necessity to forgive.

A typical ministry dialogue at this state might take the following form:

The person objects vehemently, "But I *can't* forgive him!"

"I know. But are you willing to be made willing?"

"But I don't *feel* like I can forgive!"

A good reply to that is, "*We* are not concerned with feelings at this point. You've told the Lord and me all about those, and that's good. But right now we are talking about choices. Forgiveness is not a feeling; it's a choice to give assent to Christ's work on the cross. Jesus honors that choice. It is He who accomplishes forgiveness through you. Forgiveness depends upon His power, not your ability to change what you feel." We have sometimes added, "Do you want that one who molested you to win? If you don't forgive him, he will have succeeded in destroying you. Not forgiving him will destroy your life far more than his."

If the person consents to the prayer minister's direction, prayer can be as simple as, "Lord, we are asking You to enable the heart of this wounded child to forgive." Or, if we are praying with an adult who was wounded in childhood, "Lord, enable this one as an adult to forgive, and to forgive from within the place in the heart that held the wounds as a child."

Following the prayer, it is good for the person to verbalize for himself or herself, "Lord, I choose to forgive."

The choice to forgive must be made over and over each time we become aware that we are again entertaining negative emotions. How will the person know when forgiveness has been accomplished? When she can think of the abuser with compassion, seeing him as one who is wounded, confused, sick, and sinful—one for whom Christ died and one whom God loves. When she can encounter him on the street and feel ill for *his* sake, not for her own. When the person can pray with a willing and glad heart for the abuser's forgiveness, deliverance, healing, and blessing.

How shall she know that she is healed? When she is no longer a prisoner of old defensive habit patterns. When she begins to enjoy rather than endure life. When she begins to love herself and know that she is OK, though imperfect. When she can look back on her hurtful experiences with sweet sorrow rather than shudders. When she feels grateful for everything the Lord has written on her heart through her struggles. "Since He Himself was tempted in that which He has suffered, He is able to come to the aid of those who are tempted" (Heb. 2:18). So it is with us. Our Lord enables us to forgive and heals our wounds, not by erasing our memories of what has happened, but by transforming the way we relate to those memories so that we are equipped in a beautiful and powerful way to minister to others who have experienced similar traumas.

FORGIVENESS RECEIVED AND PRAYER FOR CLEANSING

In chapter 2 we discussed varieties of guilt sexually abused people assume. They need to be told *unequivocally* that they are not responsible for the molestation. Shearer and Herbert instruct us as follows:

> Gradually introduce a "re-framing" perspective tailored to the individual. Victims of incest may inappropriately attribute adult motives and resourcefulness to themselves in their memories of the experience. Repeatedly reminding these patients of a child's need for affection and protection by adults "who know better" gradually re-frames inappropriate self-blame and reveals the true nature of the relationship.[1]

I agree, but I would add one thing more. I have found that many people can be told again and again that they are not guilty, that what they are feeling is a false guilt, but *guilt feelings* may still persist. I have continued to "re-frame" their perspective in a manner similar to that described above. But in many cases, especially those in which distinctions between real and false guilt remain blurred in the mind and emotions of the abused, we have simply met people where they are in regard to their guilt feelings and have said in prayer, "In the name of the Lord Jesus Christ I forgive you for every part of your participation in those violations of your person and in every consequence of those experiences." We use the words "In the name of…" because Jesus has authority to forgive. We use the first person "I forgive…" because Jesus has given Christians authority to forgive as the first evidence of receiving the Holy Spirit. (See John 20:22–23.)

To say "*I* forgive" as well as "*Jesus* forgives" communicates also that although we have heard about the awful things that happened, we are still accepting, loving, liking, and valuing them and choosing to stand with them. They have felt isolated, as though they have become unacceptable because of what has happened to them. People may well believe that God forgives them—but still need human love and acceptance.

As the Lord prompts, we pray vividly, "Jesus, we ask You to pour Your streams of living water all over her and into every cell of her being. Thank You, Lord, that Your living water is washing her white as snow. Every bit of defilement is being carried away. Thank You, Lord, for making her squeaky clean and new."

If we sense that her inner being is not yet accepting the message, we may describe warmth and soap being added to the water, and then ask the Lord to soak her in it. Many Christians may be more accustomed to praying about washing "by the blood of Jesus," but because they feel so bloodied already, "blood" is often not a positive reference for the sexually abused. Water is a much more appropriate image and just as biblical: "And since we have a great priest over the house of God, let us draw near with a sincere heart in full assurance of faith, having our hearts sprinkled *clean* from an evil conscience and our *bodies washed with pure water*" (Heb. 10:21–22, emphasis added). We pray aloud with her as long as the Lord inspires the prayer and until we sense that she is relaxing and receiving the content of the prayer as her personal reality.

PRAYER FOR SEPARATION OF HER SPIRIT FROM THAT OF THE ABUSER

It is impossible for one person to touch another only physically. Our personal spirit is not poured into our body like water into a container. Our personal spirit gives life to our body (James 2:26) and flows through all its cells. Therefore, when we touch another, our spirit is also involved.

> Or do you not know that the one who joins himself to a harlot *is one body with her*? For He says, '*The two will become one flesh.*' But the one who joins himself to the Lord is one spirit with Him. Flee immorality. Every other sin that a man commits is outside the body, but the immoral man sins against his own body. Or do you not know that your body is a temple of the Holy Spirit who is in you, whom you have from God, and that you are not your own? For you have been bought with a price: therefore glorify God in your body.
>
> —1 CORINTHIANS 6:16–20,
> emphasis added

God has created husbands and wives to become one flesh in holy union (Gen. 2:24; Eph. 5:31). He has so built a man that in union with his wife his spirit reaches out to enfold, protect, and nurture her. A woman is built to embrace and nurture her husband.

When two become one flesh in *un*holy union, their spirits reach out *to latch on* because that is what they were created to do. Adulterers and fornicators meet in sinful perversion of God's intent. They have not been given His permission of blessing in marriage and cannot complete one another in holiness. Their union tells lies one to the other about who they are and causes them to carry confusion within them from their coming together.

If a person has lain with many partners, his/her spirit's focus and energies are scattered, seeking the many with whom he/she was joined, and it has become impossible to bond with only one. Therefore there is a need, wherever there has been an unholy union, or worse, a molestation, to pray that the Lord Himself will wield His sword of truth to separate the personal spirit of the one from the other so that each can be free to be wholly given and present to his or her own mate. Following the guidance of the Holy Spirit, we have also prayed, directing the personal spirit in the name of Jesus to forget the union. The mind will never forget—for humility and compassion's sake—but the spirit needs to be set free to "forget" the latching on. Many for whom we have prayed in this way have exclaimed, "I feel so *together*. I didn't realize how scattered I was!"

The prayer is also effective for the one who was molested even if she did not experience full intercourse. It is common for victims of childhood exploitation to struggle with extremely ambivalent feelings toward the adults involved, especially father figures. Every child needs to feel specially chosen and loved. An abused child may have been emotionally manipulated by the lie that sexual fondling was a special sort of caring, convinced by that not to resist and to keep their "little secret." As she matured, she may have become able to decipher the truth and then violently reject sexual advances. But there may yet remain a deposit of confusion in her spirit that only prayer can reach, an unwanted remaining identification of her spirit with the one who molested her.

COMFORT AND HEALING FOR DEEP WOUNDS—REPROGRAMMING THE INNER COMPUTER

"I will be here for you" is a message that needs to be communicated verbally continually and confirmed in action. A victim of abuse feels she has been totally abandoned in her time of need and may be plagued by childish delusions that possibly she *should* have been rejected because of "bad things" inside that drew hurt to her. Her belief that she drew it to herself, that somehow she caused the hurt she endured, is one reason it is not uncommon for a victim to declare hatred toward her abuser and later speak momentarily in his defense when she hears others speaking ill of him.

She feels to a great extent isolated and rejected, even as an adult. Because of her damaged and crippled self-esteem, it is difficult for her to believe that she retains anything of blessing to contribute to a relationship. She finds it difficult to trust the motives of anyone's intentions or their promises. Therefore, if you make a promise to "be there" for her sake, *do it!* Expect to be tested regarding your sincerity and availability. *Be prepared to live what you say as best you can.*

One study of father-daughter incest showed that more than half of the women in the studied sample had a history of major depressive disorder, more than one-third had attempted suicide, and one-fifth had engaged in significant substance abuse.[2] The importance of faithfulness, integrity, and purity of motives in ministry must not be considered lightly. *Your trustworthiness may mean life to someone—your lack of integrity, death.*

Those who minister healing must *be there* for the wounded with *tenderness and respect.*

> But we proved to be gentle among you, as a nursing mother tenderly cares for her own children. Having thus a fond affection for you, we were well-pleased to impart to you not only the gospel of God but also our own lives, because you had become very dear to us…how *devoutly and uprightly and blamelessly we behaved* toward you believers; just as you know how we were exhorting and encouraging and imploring each one of you as a father would his own children.
>
> —1 THESSALONIANS 2:7, 11,
> emphasis added

One who has been sexually exploited by one she trusted, and is now daring to experience our friendship and/or ministry, is profoundly affected by how "devoutly and uprightly and blamelessly" we behave toward her. If some of her sharing seems difficult to believe, we must not add to her loss of self-esteem by challenging her credibility or by questioning her too explicitly. There will be time enough later for her to sort facts from fiction. We who minister to the sexually abused must keep our hearts pure from judging her and respond with patient understanding if our words or actions are misinterpreted or unreasonable demands are put upon us. We are called to *comfort* the afflicted.

> Blessed be the God and Father of our Lord Jesus Christ, the Father of mercies and God of all *comfort*; who *comforts* us in all our affliction so that we may be able to *comfort* those who are in any affliction with the *comfort* with which we ourselves are *comforted* by God....our *comfort* is abundant through Christ.
> —2 CORINTHIANS 1:3–5,
> emphasis added

Understanding and unconditional acceptance are themselves comforting. As we "weep with those who weep" (Rom. 12:15), the sorrowful are no longer isolated in their grief. There is restorative power in prayers for the balm of the Holy Spirit to be poured in to heal the deep lacerations and bruises of the inner man. As we bear burdens of another (Gal. 6:2) through that kind of prayer, the other is not crushed under the load of pain she still carries. "[Love] bears all things, believes all things [for the wounded one who cannot yet believe in herself or anyone], hopes all things [for the one whose ability to hope for wholesome abundant life has been destroyed], endures all things [is not turned off or turned away in discouragement by the flip-flopping of the patient]" (1 Cor. 13:7).

We who minister can be effective instruments to help people *exchange truth for lies*.

Do not lie to one another, since you laid aside the old self with its evil practices, and have put on the new self who is being renewed to a *true knowledge according to the image of the One who created him.*

—COLOSSIANS 3:9–10,
emphasis added

"I am nothing but trash." "No one could love me." "Nobody can be trusted." "My life will never amount to anything." "Nobody cares." These are all lies the sexually abused have accepted as truth. As we consistently relate to them with love and care, sensitively respecting their readiness to receive, defensive walls begin to melt. Then when we say, "I like you" or "I love you," our words begin to take on more easily acceptable meanings. "You are really a beautiful person" becomes something other than an empty or manipulative phrase.

I was once talking with a young woman concerning the destructive behavior of running away from home and engaging in promiscuity. She responded with an impassioned cry, "I've always been a tramp and I always will be!" Her father had molested her from the time she had been in primary grades, and when his sin was discovered, he would not acknowledge his guilt. Instead, he projected it onto her by saying, "The little tramp wouldn't leave me alone! I couldn't help myself!"

She had only wanted hugs from her daddy. But she accepted his lie and finally began to act on it when peer pressure made it difficult to resist. I said to her, "No, that is *not* who you are, and I don't believe it is what you *want* to be."

She argued, "You can't change the past! The sweet little girl I used to be is gone. Don't expect me to be anything different—ever!"

Then she topped off her outburst with a flood of tears and the greatest lie of all: "I *like* the way I am!"

I repeated, "You are not a tramp. You may have been trying to act like one. But that is not who you are, and you aren't happy with what you've been doing. The essence of the beautiful one God created you to be is still there, inside of you, underneath a mountain of anger and hurt. I know it's scary, but God wants you to let Him shovel the load off. He wants to do a resurrection job, to give you a *new* start. Nothing has to remain the ugly way it was."

At the moment, she was unable to embrace what I was saying, but neither was she able to reject it altogether. I knew it was a fearful thing for her to consider relinquishing her anger and hate. Anger and hate had become the only things she could identify as her protection to keep everyone at a "safe" distance. She ran away again for a while. But when she returned, it was with a hug that *she* initiated.

When the opportunity is present and the person permits you to pray, it is effective to speak directly to the victim's inmost being:

> *In the name of Jesus I break the power of the lies you have accepted—that you are worthless, bad, ugly, forever ruined and lost, and unredeemable. I say to you in the name of Jesus, who is truth, that you are beautiful, made in the beginning by the breathing of the holy breath of God into you to give you life. God doesn't make junk. You are now and always have been His priceless treasure. When you were in pain, Jesus hurt with you. He wants to take you right now into His arms as a little lamb and tell you how precious you are to Him. "Like a shepherd He will tend His flock, in His arm He will gather the lambs, and carry them in His bosom; He will gently lead the nursing ewes" (Isa. 40:11). He wants to lead you beside still waters and restore your soul (Ps. 23:2–3). It is never too late for you to be fulfilled in all that God intended for you to be. Come, Lord Jesus, carry this one and nurture her until her identity in You is written indelibly on her heart.*

In chapter 3 we noted that *inner vows* made in childhood in response to sexual abuse, though forgotten, serve later as powerful controlling and blocking mechanisms to cause sexual dysfunction in marriage. Such vows can be *broken in prayer by authority*. Jesus said, "Truly I say to you, whatever you shall bind on earth shall be bound in heaven; and whatever you loose on earth shall be loosed in heaven" (Matt. 18:18).

The prayer is simple:

> *In the name and authority of Jesus, I break on His cross the power of the inner vow. And I loose you from bondage to fear. Set her free, Lord, to come forth to meet and bless her husband as You designed her to.*

The one for whom the prayer was said must practice walking in what the Lord has made possible. She needs to *discipline* herself to exercise her new gift of power in the Lord to make free choices. "I *choose life!*" "*I choose not to flee* back into my old habit patterns." "*I will* be open and vulnerable." "The Lord *is* my shield." "I am the *best* gift the Lord has made to bless my husband, and by His grace I will be that."

A beautiful lady, Anna, to whom we ministered inner healing because of her having been molested as a child, experienced tremendous positive change in her feelings about herself and in her ability to relate to others and to God. Her deep wounds were healed, forgiveness was complete, and inner vows were broken. She had become aware of many defensive habit structures she had developed in order to survive emotionally. We prayed with her, "Lord, *bring those practices in her old man to death on the cross.*" (See Colossians 3.)

Why did we have to pray that her practiced habits be crucified? Anna was a Christian. It would seem that Jesus had already accomplished that for her and in her. Indeed He had. But she had not yet let go of the old way that had been structured into her before she became a Christian and had not yet built into herself by practice the new way of Jesus.

Consider carefully the following scriptures:

He Himself bore our sins in His body on the cross, *that* we might die to sin and live to righteousness; for by His wounds you were healed.

—1 PETER 2:24,
emphasis added

Our old self was crucified with Him, *that* our body of sin might be done away with, that we should no longer be slaves to sin; for he who has died is freed from sin.

—ROMANS 6:6–7,
emphasis added

But if the Spirit of Him who raised Jesus from the dead dwells in you, He who raised Christ Jesus from the dead will also give life to your mortal bodies through His Spirit who indwells you. So then, brethren, we are under obligation, not to the flesh, to live according to the flesh—for if you are living according to the flesh, you must die; *but if by the Spirit you are putting to death the deeds of the body, you will live.*

—ROMANS 8:11–13,
emphasis added

When Jesus died on the cross, He accomplished a finished work (John 19:30). When Anna accepted Him as Savior and Lord of her life, she became a new creature in Him, capable of making new choices that He would empower. When we prayed that her old habit structures be brought to death on the cross, she chose to specifically renounce all of her familiar flight patterns as sinful self-protection and to trust the Lord to be her defense. She grew into her new freedom as she exercised daily discipline to "reckon" an old structure as dead on the cross and to choose the new life that the Lord has made available.

Romans 6:11–14 clearly says that we are not to go on presenting ourselves to the sinful ways of our old man; rather, we are to present ourselves to God as those alive from the dead. We are enabled to fulfill that command by the power of Christ's death and resurrection and by our crucifixion with Him (Gal. 2:20; 5:24). We "die daily" (1 Cor. 15:31) as we renounce, in His power, our old habit patterns and choose to walk in a new way. Old habit patterns have a way of popping up unexpectedly. We practiced them for so many years that they have become a part of our automatic response system. Once crucified, they have no claim on us. But we must declare that death each time the old way is triggered, until at last the new way is securely established.

Anna's husband was a gentle, kind, patient, and affirming man who had supported and encouraged her throughout the healing process. But when he made love to her, old thoughts and feelings would rise in her. She would experience flashbacks and panic-filled thoughts like, "This is nasty!" "I have to get out of here!"

She overcame the paralysis of fear by catching herself at the onset: "*No!* That died on the cross with Jesus. *I will* open to my husband. Thank You, Lord, for Your enabling power and grace." The discipline remained a struggle for about three weeks. And then came blessed victory.

ROOTING AND GROUNDING IN LOVE

Prayer ministers, relatives, and friends who show forth God's unconditional love provide the *beginning* of healing. The healing itself is accomplished by the Lord as *He* is invited in prayer to do His good works. But every person must take hold of his/her own healing and walk in it; no one can do that for another. However, continuing intercession and loving friendship are essential for support. In Ephesians 3 we are provided an example by Paul, as he says:

> For this reason, I bow my knees before the Father...that He would grant you, according to the riches of His glory, to be *strengthened with power through His Spirit in the inner man*; so that Christ may dwell in your hearts through faith; and that you, being *rooted* and *grounded* in love, may be able to comprehend with all the saints what is the breadth and length

and height and depth, and to know the love of Christ which surpasses knowledge, that you may be filled up to all the fullness of God.

—EPHESIANS 3:14–19,
emphasis added

A friend of ours who owns a tree nursery explained to us the difference between being rooted and being grounded. A tree may be rooted in the ground, placed in position to grow as its roots drink nurture. But unless the soil possesses the consistency to hold the roots and the nutrients to feed them, the tree cannot develop properly and will be subject to every wind and plague. "Grounding" refers to that quality of soil that grips the tree, feeds it, and holds it in place. People are like that, needing both *rooting and grounding* in Jesus as *He* ministers through His body, the family of God.

For even though I am absent in body, nevertheless I am with you in spirit, rejoicing to see your good *discipline* and the *stability* of your faith in Christ. As you therefore have received Christ Jesus the Lord, so walk in Him, *having been firmly rooted and now being built up in Him and established in your faith,* just as you were instructed, and overflowing with gratitude.

—COLOSSIANS 2:5–7,
emphasis added

The length of the healing process depends upon both the quality of ministry and the response of the wounded. The Lord always yearns to "comfort all her waste places" and make "her desert like the garden of the LORD." As we call upon Him, "joy and gladness will be found in her, thanksgiving and sound of a melody" (Isa. 51:3).

We have rejoiced with many who, though devastated as children, have received "a garland for ashes." Planted in good soil by the Lord, they have indeed grown to be called "oaks of righteousness" (Isa. 61:1–3).

MINISTRY TO LITTLE CHILDREN

When parents have discovered that molestation has occurred, either by recognizing telltale symptoms in their little child or because the child has been able to make it known to them, they need to know what can be done.

Do not:

Blame, scold, disbelieve, overlook, minimize the seriousness of the situation, or become overwrought in the presence of the child.

Do:

1. Ask questions sensitively and matter-of-factly to obtain the history. Be careful not to allow value judgments and personal angers to add freight to your questions, and by that, frighten the child into silence.

2. Find out when the molestation occurred, where, and under what circumstances. Was it a one-time happening? How often did it happen? Is it presently continuing? (Note: If evidence needs to be gathered for a court case, allow a professional counselor—preferably court appointed or recognized—to be the first to question the child. Such experts are skilled at obtaining clear and exact answers that can be used as evidence. They are also skilled at avoiding the kinds of questions that can cause answers to appear biased.)

3. Ask the child how she or he felt about the molestation. Did it hurt? Did it feel good?

4. Teach. Caution. Pray for healing and forgiveness.
   (a) If the child replies that it felt good, the parent needs to explain that God made us to enjoy the sexual feelings that we have in our bodies, but that is not for

any of us as little children. Our bodies are beautiful and wonderful, and God has given us private parts that He wants us to share only with a husband or wife someday. Tell the child that if someone has touched any private parts or asked that he/she touch his, that person has made a big mistake. Define "private parts." Distinguish "good touches" (clean, wholesome hugs and kisses) from "bad touches" that invade their private parts. Teach him that he can and must say no to anyone who wants to touch wrongly, no matter who they are or what they say. Children need to know that it is all right to say no to an authority figure in this kind of situation. Urge the child to tell you immediately if he or she is approached again.

(b) If the child says that it hurt and/or he/she is angry, the parent needs first to express sympathy and concern. Provide a simple vocabulary of feeling words, such as sad, angry, or afraid. Assure the child that whatever he or she feels is normal and that you feel with him or her. Then pray, asking Jesus to heal the hurt and enable the child to forgive. Little children are amazingly pliable and willing to forgive. However, we caution parents not to force young children to forgive before they are ready. We especially caution not to have them directly confront a molester; the experience is too traumatic.

5. Promise the child that you will protect him/her. Do it. See to it that the molester is removed from the home; prevent opportunity to repeat the abuse. Do not remove the child from the home. He or she needs the love and support of the remaining parent (or both parents if neither of them was the perpetrator) and from siblings and other primary people, such as a live-in grandparent. An abuser is compulsive. He or she *will* do it again if left in place. The wounded one and other children

remain at risk if an abuser is not removed from the home. (This same advice is repeated on page 106, but we state it here so strongly and repeat it there because it is so important and so often not believed and followed.)

6. If the child squirms and tries to get away from you while you are talking and praying, let him/her go. Never force, but come back to it again as soon as you sense that the child is more receptive.

7. A molested child may have nightmares. Pray positive, affirmative prayers at bedtime. "Thank You, Jesus, that You are here watching and protecting. Thank You that we can go to sleep knowing that You will take care of us all night and we can rest in Your love. Thank You for the angels You send to watch over Your children" (Ps. 34:7; 91:11).

Some time ago John and I were hosted by an especially beautiful young family. The mother had been a childhood victim of abuse, and she and her husband had adopted three sexually abused children. Because these Christian parents have been there themselves, they know how to love their wounded children. Through them these little ones are becoming whole and learning the wonderful love of Father God.

God has garlands to give instead of our ashes, the oil of gladness instead of mourning, and in all this, He is glorified because only He can take a broken reed and turn it into an oak of righteousness.

Chapter 5

"MINISTRY" THAT DEVOURS
THE AFFLICTED

*There is a kind [of man] who is pure in his own eyes, yet is not
washed from his filthiness. There is a kind—oh, how lofty are his
eyes! And his eyelids are raised in arrogance. There is a kind of man
whose teeth are like swords, and his jaw teeth like knives, to devour
the afflicted from the earth, and the needy from among men.*

PROVERBS 30:12–14

THIS CHAPTER IS NOT INTENDED TO CONDEMN ANYONE FOR
either ignorant or arrogant errors in ministry to the sexually abused. *All* of us have fallen far short of Jesus's ability
to discern, love, and heal. Who can say that his motives are pure or
his perceptions completely in tune with the heart of God? *"But we
have this treasure in earthen vessels*, that the surpassing greatness of the
power may be of God and not from ourselves" (2 Cor. 4:7, emphasis
added). On the one hand we acknowledge that we are made of clay.
But at the same time we often insist on "my way" as the only way and
fail to be open to correction or new revelation the Lord might give
us directly or through the testimony of another. Or we tightly grasp
a particular technique of ministry or prayer that has "worked" for us,
confine ourselves to that, and subtly place our confidence in *what* we
"know" rather than in God *whom* we know. As my husband has said,

"We want manageable parameters, walls of thought that mean security: '*I know* what to think.' '*I know* how to feel.' '*I know* what to say.' '*I know* how to act.' '*I* am in control.'" When that happens, we can fail to be sensitive to the moving of the Holy Spirit as we minister to the abused. We may then *unwittingly wound* them with our counsel, "like swords, and…like knives, to devour the afflicted…and the needy" (Prov. 30:14).

There is a second and much more grievous kind of wounding some prayer ministers have inflicted, *not* altogether unwittingly, upon the sexually abused:

> These are springs without water, and mists driven by a storm, for whom the black darkness has been reserved. For speaking out arrogant words of vanity they entice by fleshly desires, by sensuality, those who barely escape from the ones who live in error, promising them freedom while they themselves are slaves of corruption; for by what a man is overcome, by this he is enslaved.
>
> —2 PETER 2:17–19

More than a few times we have been called to minister to women who have been devastated by counselors who tried to heal sexual problems with perverted brands of sex therapy that totally blaspheme authentic healing ministries. The pornographically horrifying tales we have heard have profoundly grieved the Lord and us.

It is fairly easy for those of us who are *not* victims of molestation to discern *unwitting* error in ministry from *intentional* opportunistic abuse. But those who are still suffering from sexual violation find it difficult to distinguish the *effects* of insensitive error from the *effects* of abuse by prayer ministers. They experience fresh wounding in their unhealed wounds and may wander away in the pain of disillusionment and futility.

The following text consists of excerpts from a letter I received from a woman who attended a seminar where I spoke briefly on the subject of sexual abuse. Her remarks express very well the sort of testimony we have heard from *many* over the years, and she graciously granted us permission to print her letter.

> I feel a need to comment on your talk on sexual abuse at the seminar last week. It was difficult to sit through, being an incest victim....The predominant emotion that kept surfacing was in response to your repeated instructions not to abandon the victim....
>
> Abandonment, aloneness are two of the biggest hurdles to overcome....After six and a half years of periodic counseling I am still struggling with risking the surfacing of those deeply entrenched emotions, and during your talk the pain brought forth by "Be there!" (counselors and friends, for the sake of the victim) was almost unbearable. Inside of me was a screaming for them to be more than instructions or nice words for myself and every other victim. But, Paula, *I have not seen this within the ministering body....*
>
> It would be wonderful to count on your blood family for help and support, but mine is not there for me and never has been. All...were involved in satanic worship using children. I was used from age two continuing into high school. All memory was buried. When my problems multiplied, I sought help from ministers and, finally, inner healing counselors. I briefly list what I have encountered during ministry because I am angry and sick about it!
>
> 1. I was raped by a minister who was counseling me. I froze. I could do nothing.
>
> 2. I shared the above with another minister who gave counsel. He knew my assailant and confronted him; the first man lied and said I was imagining it. The counselor called me and said I was not to bring it up again or contact him—it was finished.

3. I confessed this (*to a minister at a Christian retreat*). He said to contact him when I got home as I would need further help. I did so by letter and received a "form letter" thanking me for attending (*the retreat*) and wishing me a good life.

4. I waited several years and went to a clergyman in my area who was highly recommended. In the third visit, with others present who were helping with the ministry, he put his hand inside my blouse with anointing oil, pulled my pants down to do the same, and was sticking a crucifix in my navel to "deliver" me from something. I protested, then was yelled at, and I froze.

5. The first inner healing ministry I went to asked me to keep in contact when I went home. I did but received no reply. One of the counselors finally wrote that the head of the ministry had told everyone to leave me alone. I wrote him to apologize in case I had done something wrong. He replied that the other counselor had lied and he asked me to call him so he could explain what happened. I did, but never heard from him.

6. The next ministry: there was no contact from them when I left. I was told I should write and they'd keep in touch. Still nothing.

7. I made a trip halfway across the U.S. for ministry. I was to be there five days—one session per day. They saw me on the first day, skipped the second, and said they'd be there at 8:00 a.m. on the third. At noon they called—God had instructed them to fast for the healing of one of the counselors. They would let me know about the next day, and in the meantime they would keep in touch with me by phone. I never heard

from them and they would not answer when I called. They came to take me to the airport on day six and I voiced my hurt and anger. They were then angry with me, and I will never forget their words: "I know you're hurt, but we can't be concerned if you are or anyone else for that matter. We must get to the place of ministry the Lord has for us...." I then heard of their magnificent calling and how they would someday be ministering to huge multitudes with people being slain in the Spirit, etc. When I returned home, my husband had already been shown by the Lord what had happened, as well as four others who were interceding for me. They had all prayed for the Lord to rescue me from killing myself—and He did.

The letter followed with two more instances of her having shared with ministries her injuries and disappointments. They promised, "We will not do that to you," and then failed to follow through! Phone calls were not returned, letters not answered. Her letter continued:

Your instructions were beautiful, Paula, and very much needed. However, they are not being followed. The wounded are being re-wounded. In each case above, the Lord, at some time, brought another victim...to testify the same thing had happened to them. It was not just me. I have dealt with bitter-root expectancies, judgments, vows, etc. long ago that would cause this to happen, but the truth remains, there are some horrendous things taking place within the ministering body that are hindering the healing and wholeness of God's children. The Lord categorized what I have witnessed as follows: 1. lying, 2. busyness—so strong that the wounded are being treated like cattle herded into boxcars, 3. encompassing the whole thing—*PRIDE*. Also, in the arena of inner healing it is so easy to get off base with the laws—cause and effect—that a minister can, with clear conscience, *blame* the counselee with "you deserve it." And especially with incest victims, they eat it right up. I think Jesus is grieved!...It is far too easy to say, "Well, I'm not perfect," but we have not faced in anguish the hurt and harm we are giving out.

The victims of ministry abuse need prayer—and someone to listen to them. Many have turned from following Jesus; many are moving in complete distrust of Him and His ministers....

The Head of the Body cannot be separated....May we remember, *from the viewpoint of the counselee, the abused*—"As you minister to me, the words that you speak, and your actions, are showing me Jesus Christ and the Father. I do not need to become any more confused than I already am because of sexual abuse, but I will be truthful with you—the same hurt is coming from you that came from my own family, but you say it's OK since you wear a cross!"

Your talk, Paula, was different than the others you have given in this area. You were in touch deeply—and I am sorry about whatever close experience happened to bring you to this. May God's love surround you and soothe you. But keep on waving the banner! Thank you for listening to me—and not only me, but to the Lord.

As we read this letter, we found ourselves remembering the many tales of woe shared with us by those who have experienced re-wounding by well-meaning but ill-prepared and/or overzealous people. We also found ourselves wondering whom we ourselves may have injured at some time or another because of our own immaturity, ignorance, or overburdenedness. We prayed that the Lord would forgive and turn our dirty water into the finest wine for the feast. (See John 2:1–11.)

For the reader's prayerful consideration we share, from letters and reports given to us in prayer ministry, what we have learned are the most common *errors in ministry to the abused*:

1. "You've received Jesus. That's all under the blood. Now shape up and act out your new life."

My comment: Yes, when they received Jesus, the past *did* come under His blood. They *have* been born anew. They are now *babes* in the kingdom. They have already been made alive and have been raised to sit with Him in heavenly places (Eph. 2:4–6). *Positionally* they have already been made perfect (Heb. 10:14, NIV: "Because by one sacrifice he has made perfect forever…"), but *progressively* their lives are still coming to reflect that reality (v. 14 continued: "…those who are being made holy [perfect]"). *Experientially* they have yet to "work out" their new salvation (Phil. 2:12) and "grow in respect to salvation" (1 Pet. 2:2) in order to "lay hold" (Phil. 3:12) of the inheritance Jesus has made available to them by the finished work of His death and resurrection. They desperately want to experience new life, but they have only a foggy notion of what that new life is all about. What they have learned in pain heretofore, though positionally dead, still speaks loudly to them because they have not yet *lived* enough life in the Lord Jesus. Their only truly effective points of reference are those that were formed before they received Him.

Sam, who had never been able to hold a steady job or successfully complete any kind of project or responsibility, came to the Lord. He committed himself wholeheartedly to Jesus and for the first time began to feel like there could be some purpose for his life. He had a new heart to work: He no longer called in sick just because he didn't "feel" like showing up. He disciplined himself to be on time. As he began to care about quality of workmanship, his work habits improved. But because of the attitudes he had developed in reaction to a critical and abusive father, he continued to have trouble with his supervisor. It always seemed to him that unfair demands were being placed on him and preferential treatment was given to men whose work was inferior to his. Others who were newer on the job were chosen for advancement, with no explanation as to why he had been bypassed. He struggled with anger and managed to control himself fairly successfully while at work, but he exploded easily and quickly when his authority was challenged at home or when anything was said that sounded even remotely like criticism. Sam's born-again experience was real; he was indeed a new creature in Christ. But he had yet to appropriate Christ's healing and undergo the transformation of his heart at root level in relation to his father and thus other authority figures. As Sam expressed life within the family of God, time, prayer ministry, and patient teaching were necessary to build new structures of attitude and expectation into the new creature Sam had become.

A significant breakthrough occurred for Sam late one afternoon as he played with the church's men's softball team. It was an important game, and the umpire (authority figure) made a decision that Sam rightly thought was unfair. He lost his temper and was unable to respond to the warnings of his team members: "Shut up! You'll get us in trouble!" The umpire ruled that his team forfeited the game because of his continued verbal tirades. The series was lost; the fans sat in dejected silence. Then the captain (authority) called all the team members to gather around Sam. Right there on the field Sam was confronted by authority, prayed with, prayed for, and embraced with unconditional love by every member of the team. By that he gained a new point of reference concerning his relationship with authority. Through that ministry on the ball field, our Lord laid a tangible base on which a new, godly, and enduring structure could be built in Sam.

Before Gloria, a single parent of three, had her born-again experience, she thought nothing of leaving her children alone night after night while she ran to parties. "After all," she thought, "I have to work hard all day long. Nobody is looking out for me. I've had to struggle all of my life, and I deserve to have a little fun!" When Jesus came into her life, her value system changed day by day. She began to enjoy her children and to experience a sense of fulfillment in nurturing them with her presence. She no longer dated men who were just out for a good time. Rather, when she met a new man, she found herself pondering, "What kind of father might he be?" The children responded to their "new" mom with loving gratitude and respect; discipline became easy. Then one day Gloria caught her two little boys discovering masturbation, and she was suddenly overcome with irrational fear and anger! She screamed at them with vitriolic accusations as she frantically grabbed a belt to beat them. The sister cowered behind the couch as her out-of-control mom chased the boys around the house, knocking over tables and lamps as she went.

Later, a horrified and penitent Gloria tearfully cried to her pastor, "What have I done? How could I have overreacted so?" The pastor tried to be kind but did no more than reiterate the "Shape up—you know Jesus" message she had heard from the pulpit so many times before. The pressure to "be Christian" without benefit of ministry to get at the roots of why it was so difficult fueled her anxiety and drove her to repeated abuse of her children. She felt her reputation was at stake with every naughty thing they did, and her abusive discipline drove them to excesses.

Finally Gloria came to us in desperation, and the Lord very quickly revealed what her boys' sexual activity had triggered in her. As a little girl she had been fondled by a teenage boy in the neighborhood. When her parents discovered what had happened, she was blamed for the incident, shamed, whipped, and threatened with the wrath of an angry God. After we had prayed that she be enabled to forgive, we asked the Lord to heal her wounded spirit and nailed that old fearful and condemning point of reference to the cross of Christ, and she was set free.

To demand that people immediately perform because they have been born again is as ridiculous as yelling over the crib of a newborn baby, "Get out of that bed! There's work to do here!" Spiritual babes *must* have love, nurture, prayer, and patient teaching, especially those who have experienced trauma. Only then are they enabled to grow into the fullness of who they are. Insensitive religious demands put them under condemnation and drive them to hopelessness.

2. "That's in the past. Forget it!"

My comment: It is in the past in the sense that Jesus has been crucified for it on His cross. It no longer has a claim on a person's life. There are two aspects to crucifixion. *"I have been crucified* with Christ;

and it is no longer I who live, but Christ lives in me..." (Gal. 2:20, emphasis added). And Galatians 5:24, "Those who belong to Christ Jesus *have crucified* the flesh with its passions and desires" (emphasis added). Galatians 2:20 expresses the passive voice; Galatians 5:24 expresses the active voice. In the first we only receive what has been done *for* us. In the second *we* act to effectively and specifically call to death what Jesus has slain.

Some quote Philippians 3:13, claiming that it tells Christians to forget what lies behind and reach forward to what lies ahead. However, this verse is not talking about our personal past. Paul is saying that he is choosing to forget about that which he used to take pride in (circumcised on the eighth day...a Hebrew of Hebrews, and so on [v. 5]). But even if the verse did refer to our past, nothing is ever forgotten either by ignoring or suppressing it. If that is all we do, it will remain in the "treasure of [our] heart" (Luke 6:45) to drive us from deep inside and possibly to spring up someday as a "root of bitterness" to cause trouble and defile others (Heb. 12:15). Thus, we only look to the past to find the starting points of what is still happening in the *present*. The Lord would have us *recognize* that ongoing pattern of sin, *confess* it, *crucify* it in prayer in His power, *renounce* it, *reckon* it as dead, and *give it to Him*. Then it can truly be forgotten, no longer carried as hidden baggage.

If the demands of points 1 and 2 above have been presented without ministry to enable a person to fulfill them, the one who made those demands would do well to apply to himself the words of Jesus: "Woe to you lawyers as well! For you weigh men down with burdens hard to bear, while you yourselves will not even touch the burdens with one of your fingers" (Luke 11:46).

"You can do it if you try hard enough." Such demands set people into fleshly striving. The probability is that the wounded are already exhausted from striving. They need healing by the *applied* blood and the cross of Jesus. Insensitive demands are likely only to cause them to conclude, "Christianity doesn't work—at least not for me."

3. "You have a demon of lust..."

And the prayer minister proceeds to exorcise what might never have been demonic! My comment: I do not mean to say that the presence of demonic influence is never to be considered. I do say emphatically that Christians must be careful not to approach every problem as though it were first a case necessitating deliverance. Such things as lust, fear, anger, hatred, and so on are emotions that, when repeatedly acted upon, become character traits, habitual structures within a person's *flesh*. If he/she stubbornly practices fleshly habits, those structures may indeed provide housing for some demonic entity.

We appreciate the insight our son Mark has shared with us on this subject. He says that if a person has not known or chosen to put on the full armor of God (Eph. 6:13–17), he *will* wear some other kind of armor. Either we wear God's armor consciously, through prayer and relationship with Him, or we wear our own fleshly armor. It is not possible to wear no armor at all. Since nature abhors a vacuum, to the degree that trust in human authority and God's power and faithfulness have been shattered, a person who is hurt or threatened will build his own defense mechanisms, which are self-made armor. A demon may then be attracted and will mold itself in the shape of those defense mechanisms to "help" the person practice them. A person, for instance, has said, "I'll never forgive, so that I will never be vulnerable enough to be hurt again."

That determination becomes armor instead of the breastplate of righteousness. A demon then molds itself to that and expands on it, and may even tempt the person to actually take vengeance on the unforgiven one. If more and more access is given through stubborn vengeance on the unforgiven one, a demon may enter the person to inhabit his/her house of character. Before that time, the demon is only attached to part of his armor. A person's fleshly armor separates him/her from others and from God, especially if a demonic entity has become molded to it. John and I have been called countless times over the years to minister in areas of deliverance. But we do not cast out flesh. Fleshly attributes must go to the cross. Demons are to be cast out.

If a demon has been inhabiting a house of flesh, and the house is dismantled through prayer, the demon will have to leave. Sometimes eviction happens as an automatic outcome of bringing an old structure to death on the cross and filling the person's inner being with the light and love of Jesus. To bring an old structure to death, the person must repent of practices in his flesh and disavow the armor in which he trusted. When this has been done, the demon no longer has a place to live or armor to mold itself to.

Sometimes we are called upon to express our authority in the name of Jesus to cast *out* a demon directly. More often it is appropriate to pray for cleansing from the defilement of a demonic spirit that has been "hanging around the door" as it were, creating an oppressive, threatening, or accusing atmosphere. In Jesus's authority we command it to leave the premises.

How can we know the difference between actual inhabitation and merely being oppressed by something "hanging around"? By receiving and exercising the *Holy Spirit's gift of discernment* in each case.

Too often when discernment has accurately indicated the presence of a demon, the exorcist has cast it away without knowing that the house of character must be dealt with as well. What then happens is described by Jesus:

> When the unclean spirit goes out of a man, it passes through waterless places seeking rest, and not finding any, it says, "I will return to my house from which I came." And when it comes, it finds it swept and put in order. Then it goes and takes along seven other spirits more evil than itself, and they go and live there; and the last state of that man becomes worse than the first.
>
> —Luke 11:24–26

When we hear excited testimony, "We cast out 265 demons!" and there has been no testimony that structures of habit patterns in the house of flesh have been dealt with, we know that Satan probably has been given a playfield. He will willingly lose battle after battle if it means he will be granted center stage and, later, a house to return to.

If the one who ministers *falsely* assumes that a demon of lust is present and prays to cast it out, the person receiving ministry will be no freer than before. Consequently he/she may feel accused, misunderstood, and abused, or hopelessly in bondage to the devil.

Often what the prayer minister identifies as lust in the sexual abuse victim is not that at all. Dr. David Peters explains a dynamic that frequently expresses in what he calls the "latency-age group" (children between six years of age and adolescence).

> Sexualized behavior and extensive knowledge of sexual facts and terminology are important indicators of abuse.... But added to these important factors is the appearance of seductive behavior on the part of the victim during this stage. Since these children have learned at home that the only sure way to gain attention and affection is to relate sexually, *it is very common for them to behave seductively toward both peers and adults.*
>
> Such behavior may also serve the function of providing these children with a measure of control over their lives. It allows them, at least in one area, to be the aggressor rather than the passive victim. For whatever reason such behavior is adopted, *it seems to be a common phenomenon among female victims in this age division and is often carried over into the adult victim's life.*[1]

These remarks by Dr. Peters caused my spirit to leap in recognition of truth. I had observed such behavior in children and adults and had puzzled about what in sexually abused young teenage girls seemed to be *inordinate* preoccupation with sexual themes and *compulsive* flirtation. I had identified it primarily as a need for love and sometimes with self-destructive tendencies related to a lack of esteem and self-loathing. But this insight provided a new dimension of understanding. I had known with certainty that we were most often not dealing with lust, and that *to treat it as such, especially as a demon of lust, could be extremely harmful to very fragile, needy people.*

I once observed a gifted prayer minister as he responded in a very sensitive and constructive way to the seductive behavior of one young teenage girl who had come to him for ministry. She was extremely attractive and tended to relate flirtatiously to males of all ages. He had won her confidence, and she expressed her appreciation with enthusiastic affection, throwing her arms around him in a hug, pressing herself against him. He immediately responded with kindness and firmness. He told her he cared about her. He was tremendously glad that she was coming to life. But he respected her too much to allow her to express her feelings of gratitude and friendship in an inappropriate physical way that could arose sexual responses. His gentle loving rebuke was at the same time affirming. By it he drew clear wholesome boundaries for her without communicating rejection and gave her a safe resting place in his trustworthiness.

> And the Spirit of the LORD will rest on Him, the spirit of wisdom and understanding, the spirit of counsel and strength, the spirit of knowledge and the fear of the LORD. And He will delight in the fear of the LORD, and *He will not judge by what His eyes see, nor make a decision by what His ears hear*; but with righteousness He will judge the poor, and *decide with fairness for the afflicted* of the earth.
>
> —ISAIAH 11:2–4,
> emphasis added

4. The prayer minister reads a number of scriptures to the person receiving ministry, preaches a sermon at her/him, and thinks he/she ought to change his/her behavior accordingly.

My comment: There is a time and place to quote Scripture and to give teaching about it. "The word of God is living and active and sharper than any two-edged sword, and piercing as far as the division of soul and spirit, of both joints and marrow, and able to judge the thoughts and intentions of the heart" (Heb. 4:12). But the Word of God is never to be used as a club. Bludgeoning can cause "spiritual brain damage" and postpone forever the subject's ability to understand clearly. Indiscriminate piercing by the two-edged sword of truth may cut the heart to pieces. Even proper sharing of the Word is not enough if that is *all* the minister shares. "We were well-pleased to impart to you *not only the gospel of God but also our own lives*" (1 Thess. 2:8, emphasis added). Preaching and teaching involve the prayer minister only minimally. Praying with and for—yearning for and weeping with—shares "our own lives."

5. The prayer minister does do some inner healing but too soon or insensitively—and then is bemused or offended when the person is not immediately healed.

My comment: Sometimes prayer ministers rely so much upon right knowledge concerning principles and laws that they unconsciously use them like magic to guarantee results. Our first concern must be to tune ourselves to the heart of God as best we can so that we respond obediently within His timetable for His purposes. If we attempt to restore a person to ability to function too quickly, the Lord may not be given opportunity to write on the heart of the person what He wants to write there. God performs some instant miracles, but as I see it, a miracle usually occurs for one of two reasons: first, to attract someone's attention so the Lord can start a process of deeper healing and transformation. Or, He grants a "sudden" miracle as the outcome of a great deal of undercover struggle and transformation that has made the person *ripe* to receive. In either case, we who minister are the *Lord's servants* and need to move only with His patience and sensitivity, however great a miracle He may want to work. Though Jesus knew before He came to Bethany that He would raise Lazarus from more than four days of death, He waited patiently at the edge of the village for both Martha and Mary to arrive and then took time to weep with them before He acted (John 11:30–44).

It may take longer than we would like for our prayed-for miracle to arrive. The Lord said to John and me a long time ago, "*I didn't ask you to succeed. I called you to be obedient.*" What sometimes appears to be failure may only seem so because of our anxiety to see fruit from our labors. We want to look good. Some crops take longer than others to mature. If we overwater and overfertilize to hurry growth—if in our frustration and impatience we pull a tender plant out of the ground to see how it is doing, we will likely injure and possibly kill it. "One sows, and another reaps" (John 4:37).

6. People are too busy to be bothered.

My comment: This is a tough one. There are millions of people who are wounded, sick, and dying. Each one is important. They need more than a comforting pat on the head, more than an exhortation to try harder. They need long-term relationships that will firmly root them in Jesus.

Anointed ministries are overloaded. They sometimes have more compassion than common sense and often err in taking on more than they can handle, to the exclusion of their own need for Sabbath rest and commonly to the neglect of their own families. When they are unable to fulfill their promised schedule or too worn out to be attentive and compassionate, legitimately needy people feel let down and may interpret overworked, tired responses as rejection. Not being available to talk on the phone and delays in answering mail can be seen by some as evidence of a lack of caring—especially by those who haven't had a good look at the prayer minister's load from the underside of *his* mountain of stress. A deeply caring person may run "too busy" for a long time without feeling bothered until seemingly out of the blue he begins to experience burnout. At that point, everything and everybody bothers his stretched and bruised sensitivities.

There are, of course, many empire builders who are busy administering busy work, spending much energy and time supporting causes the Lord did not initiate, attending endless numbers of meetings and "meeting" no one. People soon learn not to beat a path to the doors of such men to ask for healing. They do not have it to give.

As for those who are giving more than they were designed to give, I see only one answer. The *body of Christ* must become the unified, healing, nurturing *family of God* it is called to be.

> And He gave some as apostles, and some as prophets, and some as evangelists, and some as pastors and teachers, *for equip-ping of the saints for the work of service [leaders training and coaching the whole body to make them into "consummate artists" in ministry]*, to the building up of the body of Christ; until we *all* attain to the unity of the faith, and of the knowledge of the Son of God, to a mature man, to the measure of the stature which belongs to the fullness of Christ....speaking the truth in love, we are to grow up in all aspects into Him, who is the head, even Christ, from whom the *whole body*, being fitted and held together by that which *every* joint supplies, according to the proper working of *each individual part*, causes the growth of the body for the building up of itself in love.
>
> —Ephesians 4:11–16,
> emphasis added

"Building up" in the text above comes from the Greek word *oikodomeo*, which literally means, "to build a house." The church today must return to the New Testament pattern in which the people as the total body of the church met in the temple to worship, but during the week met "house to house" in small groups where through heart-to-heart healing relationship, they could be built into a living house of God. Today, where there is some sort of *small group structure within the church* in which *people are learning to minister effectively to one another*, there is no great outcry that the leadership is too busy to be bothered. These churches have reexamined their priorities and have chosen to become *healing* bodies rather than simply *busy* bodies. Some have become healing bodies even for their pastors.

7. Some in-depth prayer ministry and healing is done but without installing the person in a loving support group.

My comments: Ministry from a prayer minister alone will not overcome feelings of isolation. The love of Jesus alone will not restore a sense of humanly belonging. Regular participation in a group in which people know, understand, and accept you just as you are provides a context for the Lord to begin to fill waste places in the heart, raise self-esteem, and build new trust. This is especially needed by teenagers. If there is no small-group structure within the church, it is important to search for a wholesome family from whom the person can drink nurture for a while. It is not enough to bring the negative to death on the cross. Sexually abused people especially need to experience positive nurture within a family group or else they find it very difficult to sustain healing.

8. If the abuse victim is a child, sometimes prayer ministers fail to follow legal requirements established to protect the abused.

He/she is then left in the presence of the offender, vulnerable to him. My comments: Most prayer ministers agree that one of the most important factors in healing lies in the restoration of the bond between mother and daughter. For this reason it is always preferable to remove the offender rather than the victim from the home. This action also provides some measure of protection for other children in the family who might also become victims of the yet-unhealed abuser. We have ministered to numerous victims who either were taken from their homes or who voluntarily left home to avoid repeated violation and then years later discovered that the abuser had also molested one or more of their siblings.

9. The victim is told, "You must have brought this on yourself."

My comment: The sickness is the abuser's. The guilt is his. Even in cases where the victim was to some degree consenting, the load of guilt is the abuser's. He represented authority. Authority overcomes resistance, especially when the authority figure deceives the innocent with lies about the "specialness" of relationship that he says makes sexual touches "OK" or "our secret." Or when the authority figure puts emotional burdens on the immature with appeals such as, "Mommy does not love me anymore. I feel *so* bad. *I need you* to hold me and comfort me." Or when authority threatens, "If you tell anyone, this whole family will blow up, and it will be your fault."

Blame placed on sexually abused people for violations that happened in ministry or at other times (seemingly due to their bitter-root judgments and expectancies) comes from a gross misunderstanding and misapplication of the scriptures concerning sowing and reaping (as the letter quoted earlier in this chapter indicated). Bitter-root judgments and expectancies may influence a situation, but *never* should the victim be blamed or condemned!

10. The credibility of the abused is challenged.

My comment: This can throw the victim into despair and deeper isolation. "No one believes me. No one understands." Whatever thread of trust might have existed before has now become strained to the point of breaking. It will be a long time, if ever, before the abused will again expose the pain and shame of her bleeding heart.

Many knowledgeable prayer ministers and counselors have testified that in their experience, in most instances, a child will not fabricate a lie concerning sexual abuse by a parent or loved one. Except in rare instances, a child is more likely to lie to stay *out* of trouble rather than to get *into* it. She is well aware that discovery of abuse will cause horrendous upset to the entire family. When memories of trauma have already been discussed and rehashed, some details might have been distorted, so as to cause confusion in the telling of the story. We must not be critical of details that seem not to fit. These may only be misplaced. There are elements of truth in every aspect of a jumbled story. Listen. Hear. Investigate, question, and ponder information apart from the victim. Minister to the abused person, meeting her where she is. Deal with her responses to her version of the truth. Pray that the Lord will reveal the whole truth and execute His justice. Later on, the abused may begin to piece her history together more coherently and consistently.

11. Insistence that the victim relive the experience emotionally in order to be healed

My comments: Most likely the victim of sexual abuse has involuntarily relived again and again the agonies of her experience, at least in bits and pieces, waking and sleeping. If the trauma was such that she repressed all memories, we might ask the Holy Spirit to bring the experiences to light in a gentle way *as* she is ready to look at them long enough to let them go to the cross. But it is not necessary to endure an emotional wringer in order to be healed. By faith we accept Jesus as Savior. By faith we receive the baptism in the Holy Spirit. By faith we can receive healing as we invite the Lord Jesus Christ to reach to the depths of our innermost being to comfort, heal, and transform the devastation sexual abuse has caused. If a person to whom you are ministering is fighting to control emotions rushing to the surface, it is good to tell her, "Go ahead, cry—say what you're feeling. It's OK. Let your feelings live!" But if the one who ministers insists and manipulates emotionally so that she relives an experience or expresses an emotion not called for or stirred by the Lord, he may only afflict her cruelly, even though his aim is to encourage catharsis.

12. Using imagination falsely to change a hurtful remembrance

My comments: To imagine that an experience was other than the way we remember it is to ask the inner being to accept a lie. A game of "Let's Pretend" may fetch some temporary relief, but the inner being will throw it off eventually, and the abused person will be back at square one with a sense of defeat and futility. There is no substitute for the blood and cross of the Lord Jesus Christ to transform a person's heart and set her free.

Some prayer ministers rightly invite the abused, in prayer, to see Jesus standing by them, hurting and grieving for them at the time of their injury, wanting to act, but not yet invited. This is not an imagining of something contrary to fact. It is to acknowledge reality. Jesus *was* there. Envisioning His presence does *not cause* Him to be there right then as imagined. It only celebrates the reality that He *was* there. The victim could not see or experience His presence at the time of wounding—but he or she may need to know, for healing. "Can you believe that He loves you? That He was hurting for you? Can you give Him your pain now?" Many have been deeply blessed and healed by the revelation that Jesus was indeed there.

13. Using imagination falsely to get rid of an anger or hatred

My comments: We have been called on to minister to a number of people who sank into deep depression following a session in which the person who ministered told them to imagine that a pillow or block of wood represented the father who had violated. They had followed instructions to pummel the pillow as they cried, "I hate you!" Or they were directed to plunge a knife into the block of wood. Contrary to the release the minister was trying to achieve, the abused person's already existing feelings of guilt were compounded by committing acts of hatred and murder.

14. Healing wounds in an individual without sensitively probing to discover the nature of her woundedness in the context of the whole family

My comments: Sexual abuse usually occurs in families where other problems are contributing—fractured mother/father relationship, undealt-with roots of bitterness, generational inheritances, quarreling, economic stress, overcrowding, battering, alcoholism, and the like. A conscientious medical doctor will not remove one piece of gravel from an injured hand and then sew up the wound without probing to make sure there are no other hidden pieces. A good prayer minister will examine with the same thoroughness all other possible spiritual and emotional wounds.

15. Using hypnotism

Some use this method to uncover things hidden in the unconscious, even though God forbids its use (Deut. 18:10–11). (See chapter 3 for my comments.) Hypnotism is strictly forbidden.

16. Attempts to receive gifts of knowledge in sinful or insensitive ways

- Receiving a word from the Lord but blurting it out too soon. My comments: The Lord may give the prayer minister insight or revelation to ponder and pray about until the abused person's heart has been prepared to hear and respond. Fleshly zeal to share a word may rape the process or strike fear into the heart of the person, causing her to flee and shut down. "He who restrains his words has knowledge, and he who has a cool spirit is a man of understanding" (Prov. 17:27).

- Trying to receive insights by occult or psychic ways of seeing. My comment: This may open the door to direction from *un*holy spirits, resulting in polluted under-standings that add to already existing confusion—and to demonization and further wounding.

17. Demanding repentance or forgiveness when the person is not yet ready

My comment: Eventually both are necessary, but if the person is forced too soon to go through the motions to please the prayer minister, there will be no reality to the consent, and she will go away still harboring unforgiveness. Then she will hide behind the closed doors of her heart and mind, so that no one will ever see enough to challenge with accusation again.

18. Insisting that the victim talk it out with the abuser

My comment: There may be an appropriate time later for that. But it will come much later, after a great deal of healing has been accomplished in both the abused and the abuser. Premature meeting is likely to pick the scabs from emotional wounds that are still bloody and tender.

19. Taking the victim through a surface ritual of forgiveness with the offender, then insisting that the "repentant" and forgiven abuser be restored to his home immediately

My comment: Many fundamentalist Christians have done this and have blinded themselves to inevitable continuing molestation because they are convinced, "That was all taken care of. He said with tears that he is sorry. It's under the blood and he's a new creature." Such prayer ministers may respond to reports of further violation with disbelief: "She's making it up." "She's rebellious and unwilling to forgive." This error happens because of a lack of adequate understanding of the process of healing. Rightly comprehending the necessity and power of the *blood* and *forgiveness*, they fail to grasp the necessity of the application of the *cross* for death of *practices* in the heart of the abuser. They make a magic of forgiveness, expecting it to accomplish more than it can. There can be no substitute for death on the cross to long-established patterns in abusers' lives.

Many years ago a couple came to John for prayer ministry concerning their very troubled marriage. It was the husband's earnest hope that enough healing might be accomplished that their differences could be reconciled. But the wife energetically resisted every step in the process. Her attitude and manner were flippant, saucy, and disrespectful. At times she played a ridiculously seductive role in John's presence, as though to say, "We all know I'm only here at the insistence of my husband. I'll show him how far that will get him by trying to entice my prayer minister." Her attempts at seduction only disgusted John; he had to forgive silently in order to be able to continue to listen to her.

It was then revealed in the prayer ministry process that the wife had been molested as a child by her father, who was also a minister. She had largely suppressed the memories of his abuse and refused to consider that experience as an important contributor to the struggles she and her husband were now having. She continually blocked attempts to counsel and heal, until John had to discontinue ministering to them. When the wife later flaunted an adulterous relationship she had developed with one of her husband's business associates, the husband finally reluctantly concluded that reconciliation was an impossible dream and determined to divorce her.

Their divorce agreement clearly stipulated that the wife must never take their two daughters to visit in her father's home unsupervised. This was to be enforced as a protection for the girls against possible molestation by their grandfather. The wife ridiculed the need for such a ruling, and when she violated the terms of the contract, exposing the children to periods of unsupervised time with the grandfather, the husband moved to obtain custody of the children for their safety.

During the custody battle that followed, John was asked to present a deposition. He stated that the wife had admitted that her father had molested girls, even herself. He warned that there was a strong likelihood that he would molest his granddaughters if given the opportunity. He said moreover that family loyalties should not be allowed to mean that the girls' lives should be risked with a known violator; the grandfather had forfeited his rights to be with the children by his acts of sexual abuse. Other religious leaders gave depositions supporting the wife's father, saying that he was truly sorry and did not need to be counseled. Some knowingly told lies to cover the man's sin. John's warning was rejected, and the wife was again awarded custody of the children.

Many years later, the wife's father was prosecuted for sexually molesting his granddaughters and other children. Forgiveness alone is never enough!

20. Comforting only, without bringing forgiveness and the cross to bear

My comment: This will tend to establish and even entrench the victim in pity parties.

21. Allowing catharsis to become rehearsal

My comment: The grooves get deeper and deeper, and the patient may die in an emotional rut.

22. Becoming emotionally involved with the abuse victim and failing to discern a transference relationship (a condition in which a dependent person transfers loyalties and unresolved tensions from former relationships onto the prayer minister or friend who is assisting her)

My comment: A female victim of sexual abuse is perhaps the most fragile of all wounded people. Because of fractured trust, low self-esteem, loneliness, and tremendous need for loving affirmation, she is extremely vulnerable behind whatever defensive walls she has built. If she finally begins to perceive the prayer minister as one who is compassionate, kind, and understanding and begins to dare to open in trust, she may be inclined to enter into a dependent relationship. Her sense of who she is then leans too heavily upon the way the prayer minister looks at her, speaks to her, and spends unrushed time with her. The prayer minister has become to her *"the only* one who understands how I feel. No one else cares."

She craves affirmation from the one she has let into her guarded inner world, and she may relate possessively. If the prayer minister is a man, she may begin to allow herself to love him in a variety of ways—as a friend, a brother, a father. She may even entertain some romantic fantasies in relation to him. To her, he seems to be a safe object for her affections.

As the Lord ministers to her through prayer, she receives enough genuine *agape* love to strengthen her spirit with ability to begin to shift her focus from pain and wanting to die, to a desire to live. But life for her becomes too identified at the emotional level with affirmation and nurture from the prayer minister. Now she may talk about Jesus and verbalize that He is her primary source. But her relationship with Jesus has become largely represented by and communicated through the flesh-and-blood person on whom she has learned to depend for understanding, comfort, healing, and direction. Once she has entered into transference, the prayer minister may want to disengage and palm her off to someone else. But he must not peremptorily do so. An abused heart beginning to come to life can only perceive the change as another rejection. If possible, the prayer minister should walk through it with her for the sake of the abused.

It is essential that the prayer minister keep the lines of sensibility and purity in the relationship. He must stand as a paragon of virtue and integrity, girded with the laws of God, resting solidly upon the rock who is Jesus. He must view every aspect of his relationship with the abused person as a sacred trust from God. As she leans upon him with many different kinds of needs, he must die to his need to be needed. Since her dependency may feed his ego, he must continually look to the Lord for affirmation so that he does not become puffed up with pride due to his own areas of insecurity. If his relationship with his wife is in need of repair, he had better tend to it. His wife is God's gift to protect his heart. If he is in ministry as a single man, he should submit himself to close friends who can pray to keep him on track. Married or single, he needs to invite the Lord to deal with the unhealed areas of his own heart that can make him vulnerable to temptation and deception. As the victim transfers all kinds of love as friend, brother, father, or sweetheart onto him as she comes to life, he must identify the relationship clearly as transference, define it sensitively to her (if she is ready for that), and *not* allow himself to respond romantically in any way. Her *life* depends upon his *trustworthiness*, and God Himself will hold the prayer minister responsible for any violation of that sacred trust (Heb. 13:17).

The testimony shared in the letter at the beginning of this chapter was regrettably not an unfamiliar one to us. Errors abound, and transferences are dangerous. Prayer ministers should never try to make them happen. But if the abused falls into it, the prayer minister must circumspectly walk it through in the wisdom and power of the Holy Spirit. Many have set out in the strength of their flesh to minister and have fallen.

Leadership, a former publication of Christianity Today, Inc., reported:

> The research department of Christianity Today, Inc., mailed nearly one thousand surveys to pastors, and 30 percent responded.
>
> According to the results of this survey, sexual temptation among pastors is a problem—70 percent of the respondents expressed the belief that pastors are particularly vulnerable....
>
> The survey probed the frequency of behavior that pastors themselves feel is inappropriate.
>
> *Since you've been in local church ministry, have you ever done anything with someone (not your spouse) that you feel was sexually inappropriate?* The responses: 23 percent yes; 77 percent no.
>
> *Have you ever had sexual intercourse with someone other than your spouse since you've been in local church ministry?* Yes: 12 percent. No: 88 percent....
>
> *Have you ever had other forms of sexual contact with someone other than your spouse, i.e., passionate kissing, fondling/mutual masturbation, since you've been in local church ministry?* Yes: 18 percent. No: 82 percent....
>
> Those pastors who acknowledged having had intercourse or other forms of sexual contact were asked about who the other person was. The responses:
>
> 1. A counselee (17 percent)
>
> 2. A ministerial staff member (5 percent)
>
> 3. Other church staff member (8 percent)

4. A church member in a teaching/leadership role (9 percent)

5. Someone else in the congregation (30 percent)

6. Someone outside the congregation (31 percent)

These pastors were also asked about the major factors that led them to salacious relationships. The most frequent answer: "Physical and emotional attraction" (78 percent). "Marital dissatisfaction" was a distant second (41 percent).[2]

PERVERSION IN MINISTRY TO THE ABUSED

There is another kind of "ministry" that goes *far* beyond ignorance or common error. I believe it is rare. *I* would rather believe that it does not exist at all, but I cannot. The following examples describe graphically the sort of testimonies we have listened to in ministry sessions, have received in letters, and have heard from people who timidly and tearfully shared their experiences with us after hearing our teaching concerning ministry to the abused. The clear message that they have not been the only ones who have suffered violation and humiliation in therapy has been to some extent comforting and freeing. The assurance that they do not have to continue to live under a sickening weight of compounded defilement and self-condemnation has given them a measure of courage to seek healing once again. I include these examples as a warning to the abused, and especially to those in ministry positions who would take advantage of the confusion and vulnerability of abuse victims to employ hellish methods that cannot do anything but inflict pain and cause further devastation.

A type of "therapy" was reported to us by several women counseled by a minister who, though not sponsored by any Christian organization, nevertheless traded upon his church affiliation to attract trusting clients. His method consisted largely of holding on his lap (for extended periods of time) a woman who had been starved for authentic affection and/or violated sexually as a child. He would begin by playing a loving and protective Christian father role, tenderly caressing the client's shoulders and back, affirming her with compliments concerning her beauty and worth, until she began to relax into his arms. The therapy filled such a lifelong void in her that she would begin to grow more and more dependent upon the pastor's understanding assurances and touches to give her strength to handle her problems. Relationship with him supplied her with a sense of belonging and well-being in the midst of her tension-filled environment. After a number of sessions he would begin to explore and fondle sexual areas. Frequently he manifested an erection that, if she responded with resistance, he then defended as something the patient had caused by her desire or desirability. Fortunately this man was reported, confronted, and prevented from doing further harm. But we have heard of others who employed similar seductive methods and did not stop short of rape. Victims were so devastated that they retreated into months or years of fear and shame-filled silence.

We have heard tearful testimonies concerning therapists who treated frigidity by sexually arousing their clients with foreplay, then sending them home "prepared" for their husbands. Or worse, the therapist persuaded a client to participate in full intercourse with him in order to "overcome inhibitions" or to "to be instructed in the art of lovemaking." This was supposedly to equip her to be a better lover so her marriage might be saved!

The most drastically destructive treatment reported to us was a bizarre twist on regression (a method that I have already warned against in point 11). The therapist would employ varieties of methods to cause a patient to regress emotionally to the approximate age she was when she was originally sexually abused. His intent was that she should relive what happened to her in the past in order for her to become consciously and specifically aware of the hurtful details of her experiences and her feelings and responses concerning them. "Reliving" went beyond stimulating imagination and memory-recall; it often included stimulation by sexual manipulation, and patients were sometimes forced to handle the sex organs of the therapist.

Why should people who have been abused endure such treatment? They have come to the prayer minister, counselor, or therapist because they are desperate for help. They have failed to achieve any significant degree of healing and freedom by their own efforts. Now they have reached the limits of their ability to cope with inner pain, confusion, and failure to establish full, wholesome, and lasting relationships. Moreover, they realize that if their present condition continues, they are likely to lose what little life they have gained. The treatment the therapist offers offends and frightens them, but he insists, "You have to quit backing away from everything. Do you want to keep running away from life? I know what I'm doing! Do you want to miss your only chance for wholeness?" So they try to overcome the sick and fear feelings inside and tell themselves that he is the therapist and must have more wisdom than they. By the time they realize the therapist has been taking advantage of their vulnerability, they are unable to tell anyone because they are so filled with humiliation and shame. Unfortunately, reports of such sick and abusive "ministry" are usually made many years too late for the transgressor to be traced and held accountable.

Is it fair to say, as some counselors and prayer ministers have done, that these people are consenting adults and therefore guilty and responsible for what they allow? No. Adults who are still suffering severe emotional effects of childhood sexual abuse *are not to be judged to be consenting adults.* They may still be living in the woundedness and consequent distortion of childhood emotions. Later, when they are truly engaged in the healing process, they may be able to assume appropriate responsibility for having participated with faulty discernment. But hopefully by then they will be able to do so with compassion for themselves and *without self-condemnation.*

Such abusive therapy is an abomination in any circumstance. Experiences of this kind of behavior should be reported and thoroughly and quietly investigated by well-trained and perceptive authorities so that appropriate actions can be taken.

And do not participate in the unfruitful deeds of darkness, but instead even expose them; for it is disgraceful even to speak of the things which are done by them in secret.

—Ephesians 5:11–12, emphasis added

The warning to the abused is this: do not seek help from a counselor or prayer minister who is not *accountable* to any psychological or Christian association or church, no matter what kind of popular credibility he may have gained in the community.

The warning to prayer ministers who employ perverted methods is this: though you may never be reported, you delude yourself if you think that you will escape judgment.

Those who are guilty *will* be held accountable by God for their transgressions. The Old Testament presents a stern word:

Listen to the word of the LORD, O sons of Israel, for the LORD has a case against the inhabitants of the land, because there is no faithfulness or kindness or knowledge of God in the land. There is swearing, deception, murder, stealing, and adultery. They employ violence, so that bloodshed follows bloodshed. Therefore the land mourns, and everyone who lives in it languishes....My people are destroyed for lack of knowledge. Because you have rejected knowledge, I also will reject you from being My priest. Since you have forgotten the law of your God...I will change their glory into shame. They feed on the sin of My people, and direct their desire toward their iniquity. And it will be, like people, like priest; so I will punish them for their ways.

—Hosea 4:1–3, 6–9

Meanwhile, we (and most prayer ministers and pastors) persevere as best we know how in persistent application of the healing and transforming power of our Lord Jesus Christ.

Jesus said, "Pray that you may not enter into temptation" (Luke 22:40). We who are in leadership, and especially we who minister, would do well to follow that directive. We need to pray with and for one another that our areas of vulnerability might be dealt with, that we might not enter into temptation and carry the already wounded along with us.

There is forgiveness for sin. There is ministry for inner healing to transform our hearts so that we are less susceptible to temptation, delusion, and error. There is restoration in our Lord Jesus Christ. We serve a God who is much bigger than our ability to make mistakes.

Chapter 6

THE CHARACTERISTICS
OF AN ABUSER

Therefore you are without excuse, every man of you who passes judgment, for in that you judge another, you condemn yourself; for you who judge practice the same things. And we know that the judgment of God rightly falls upon those who practice such things. And do you suppose this, O man, when you pass judgment upon those who practice such things and do the same yourself, that you will escape the judgment of God? Or do you think lightly of the riches of His kindness and forbearance and patience, not knowing that the kindness of God leads you to repentance? But because of your stubbornness and unrepentant heart you are storing up wrath for yourself in the day of wrath and revelation of the righteous judgment of God, who will render to every man according to his deeds: to those who by perseverance in doing good seek for glory and honor and immortality, eternal life; but to those who are selfishly ambitious and do not obey the truth, but obey unrighteousness, wrath and indignation.

ROMANS 2:1–8

R OMANS 2:1 COULD BE SUMMED UP SIMPLY, "SINCE THERE IS NO sin that is not common to us all, if you have made a *condemning* judgment against another and have come to no repentance and forgiveness, you *will* reap the same divine judgment he reaps." Our judgments against others are a form of unforgiveness. Regarding unforgiveness, Jesus said, "But if you do not forgive men, then your Father will not forgive your transgressions" (Matt. 6:15). That is the power behind what Paul says in Romans 2. We all have the same sinful propensities in our hearts. Therefore, if we judge another, we remain unforgiven, and our propensity toward the same sin we have committed remains in our heart. The principle of increase (Hosea 8:7, "For they sow the wind, and they reap the whirlwind") ensures that we become more and more like the one we judge. In light of that, the message of Deuteronomy 5:16 takes on a far more potent meaning: "Honor your father and your mother, as the Lord your God has commanded you...that it may go well with you." If we have *not* honored our parents—*tried* to love, obey, respect, and forgive them, life will *not* go well for us.

Here are two more scriptures that highlight the same subject: "Do not be deceived, God is not mocked; for whatever a man sows, this he will also reap" (Gal. 6:7), and, "Do not judge lest you be judged. For in the *way* you judge, you will be judged; and by your standard of measure, it will be measured to you" (Matt. 7:1–2, emphasis added).

The Word of God describes the way reality works. The laws of God were not made by an angry Creator who wanted to punish His creation, but by a loving Father who was concerned to maintain order in His universe for the sake of His children. His principles and laws are impersonal and eternal, established from before the foundation of the world. Ephesians 1:3–4 says that He "has blessed us with every spiritual blessing in the heavenly places in Christ, just as He chose us in Him before the foundation of the world, that we should be holy and blameless before Him." And, "He disciplines us *for our good*, that we may share His holiness" (Heb. 12:10, emphasis added). He intended the laws of sowing and reaping to bless us. God's laws were established before sin entered the picture. When mankind chose to sin, the same laws that had been created for blessing continued to operate for negative reaping. But many Scripture references assure us that we will in no way lose our reward for the love and blessings that we sow (Matt. 10:41–42; Mark 9:41; 1 Cor. 3:8, 14; 2 Cor. 9:6; Eph. 6:8; Col. 3:24). It is not that we are forbidden to judge. We must make certain necessary judgments prior to every decision. Here are three examples of good ways of judging:

1. Secondhand smoke is damaging to my health—I will ask for a table in the far corner of the no-smoking section.

2. Mrs. T. repeats everything she hears—I will confess my faults to someone else who has learned to respect and keep confidences.

3. My husband is tired and cross today—I will give him time to rest and get refreshed before I talk to him about Billy's D in math.

These three judgments are quite different:

1. What's the matter with those self-centered, inconsiderate so-and-sos who stink up the whole atmosphere with their stupid pollution?

2. Mrs. T.'s tongue wags at both ends and in the middle. I wouldn't tell her the time of day!

3. You'd think that a kid's father would take some interest! All he ever does is come home and flop in front of that stupid television! He's *never* here when I need him!

Making these latter judgments is an almost sure guarantee that even if you don't smoke, you will just as surely pollute the coffee shop with your stinky attitude! Even if you don't join Mrs. T. in her gossip, your judgment of her will be just as cutting as hers are of others. And your husband's disinterest in his kids will be rivaled only by your disinterest in his need for some rest, as well as by your inability to read his heart to find out whether, after a little rest, he might just be the attentive father you would like him to be!

Often we fail to see the relationship between our sowing and reaping, especially when present reaping has to do with judgmental responses made to wounding that happened years ago when we were little children. But since childhood we have practiced those responses until they have colored and controlled our entire way of seeing and interpreting life (Matt. 6:22–23). All of us build powerful, unconscious, defensive coping mechanisms that provide us with a measure of safety from hurt but lock us into practices, prisons of fear, and pain that we treasure in the heart (Luke 6:45). By this we are kept from wholesome, intimate relationship with God and from people who could teach our hearts to trust and who could nurture us to grow. And thus we consign ourselves to do what has been done to us, both because of the law and because we have never really *known* any other way.

What does this have to do with the sexual abuser?

> Group profiling of molesters indicates that less than 10 percent are classifiable as "mentally ill." Most are immature, socially inadequate individuals who outwardly appear normal.[1]

Studies tell us that molesters are very often involved in service-oriented occupations and activities. It is not uncommon for them to be teachers, Scout leaders, day-care workers, ministers, youth leaders, and the like. They are often charming and intelligent people who have gained a good measure of respect in the community. They may be completely sincere in their *conscious* desires to help others. However, my observation in counseling is that often they are deeply and power-fully motivated by *unconscious*, inordinate, self-centered needs to find well-being and fulfillment *through* those whom they "serve." They have never developed the capacity to really *meet* another person in a wholesome, *mutually nurturing* relationship. *Thus they tend to try to satisfy their own hungers in nonthreatening situations where they can feel expansive and helpful but in which they are in control.*

The following is a general description of the history and character of a potential sexual abuser. There may be some persons who fit many aspects and yet have never become abusers. If this description strikes some hearts with fear, let it be that kind of holy fear that can drive them to the cross, giving the Lord an opportunity to heal areas of vulnerability. My prayer is that all who read this may begin to respond to abusers with increased understanding and compassion—not to *excuse* their sin, but to be prepared to help them to deal with it at the root level, without condemnation.

A typical molester is one who was himself wounded early in life. Perhaps he was unwanted—neither valued as a person nor nurtured by affectionate love from his parents. Perhaps he was used sexually, beaten physically, abused emotionally, or neglected. A Canadian survey found that as children, 33 percent of teenage sex abusers had been abused or neglected. An American survey put the numbers at 60 percent for physical abuse, 50 percent for sexual abuse, and 70 percent for neglect.[2]

With regard to sex abuse in particular, I have seen other estimates ranging from 30 percent[3] to as high as 85 percent! One survey has reported that 50 percent of all sexual offenders have at some time been victims of sexual assault.[4] Although statistics vary widely, an obvious pattern is emerging.

The molester may also have been deeply lacerated by continual criticisms and demands. The relationship he had with one or both parents may have been so possessive and controlling that his own true personality and character have been smothered.

But the most common trait is a feeling of inadequacy.[5] In almost every case, performance orientation was strongly built into the heart, accompanied by a powerful sense of futility. When he was a child, a molester's parents might have driven him to perfection or were extremely rejecting. It is not uncommon for such parents to have told their child, "I wish you were never born," or "You are an accident that we regret."[6] Or they may have placed him in a care-giving role, overwhelming him with the responsibility to care for others, emotionally or physically.[7] The child's life message became, "I will do everything I possibly can to earn the right to be, to be loved, and to belong. But I'm in a no-win position. I'll never make it with the people who count."

He learned to compare himself with others and found himself failing. To avoid failing in relationships, he became a loner.[8] If he did have friends, he did everything he could to please them, or he tried to impress them with heroics in sports or sexual exploits or by just being macho.[9] He grew up seeing only how others did better, not worse, than he did.[10] This may have affected his body image. He is likely to think his penis is too small, no matter what size. When asked what is normal, he cannot tell you or may cite some ridiculously large measurement he has heard from peers or has seen in pornography. It has not even occurred to him to check his assumptions against reality by observing other men in the locker room.[11] The real issue is the size of his self-esteem; he may never give himself any praise, or he may hide his shame behind boasting.[12] He may be a perfectionist who sets goals too high to achieve, like losing fifty pounds in a week. Therefore, he may tend to be a quitter.[13] Because of his drive to please, he may chose the same career as his father, even if he hates it. Or he may try to follow in the footsteps of someone he idolizes.[14]

The molester's heart was fractured from the beginning, and the cracks deepened with each blow to his self-esteem.

He soon learned that it was not only unacceptable but also actually dangerous to express his true feelings, and so he began to actively suppress what he felt in order to "play the game" in order to get by with as little trouble as possible.

He began to build defensive walls and develop ways to protect his heart. He withdrew from family activity as much as possible and shared his innermost thoughts with no one. Though he felt protected, in that no one any longer knew accurately where to "hit" him, there was yet no resting place for him.

His inner balance has been destroyed. There is no stable base inside—only fractured pieces of his "heart of stone" (Ezek. 36:26).

His instability manifests in some or all of the following ways:

1. Confused and agitated

His confusion and agitation manifest through digestive problems and disrupted sleep cycles. He feels increasing pressures of unfulfilled but unidentified needs. He is likely to find himself loaded with many tasks but without enough ability to organize his time or energies. He tends to wander in circles and finally settle on one aspect of a day's work, something he enjoys, to the exclusion of the rest of his agenda. Projects are begun, but many are never completed; time is never sufficiently accounted for. When criticisms or even suggestions for help are offered, he can perceive these only as personal attacks or threats to his private citadel. Because of all this, typically he has been released from a number of jobs over the years but has never been able to accept responsibility for his fault in the matter.

2. Impaired perceptions

He frequently manifests inability to discern, judge, and reason accurately, especially in situations where his reputation and position are involved. If another looks him in the eye, he may feel accused. Or if someone speaks to him with eyes averted, he may think the person is not being totally honest with him. If he is accused falsely and someone clearly defends him, he may be inwardly so devastated by the accusation that he fails to hear the supportive word. Within the family, he either rules as a dictator or is passive and hen-pecked.[15] If he acts as a dictator, when he does choose to be with his family, they must focus on him and his interests *exclusively*. His wife cannot be occupied with handwork while they sit to watch TV. If they are talking together, she is not allowed simultaneously to take care of a household chore. If one of the children interrupts and she responds to the child's need, he may become instantly jealous and competitive for attention. He has always had a need to be in control and is compulsively an authority on every subject, whether he is knowledgeable or not. He lives behind a veneer of poised charm and "I have it together"-ness that deceives many who have not lived with or tried to work with him.

3. Angry and judgmental

Anger and judgment are combustible driving forces within him, but they are seldom directed appropriately. He may be merely inhibited emotionally. Or he may be unable to show any emotion except anger, and even that will be minimal and overly controlled.[16] When he does openly show it, he may project his negative emotions onto whatever objects and people happen to be nearby when feelings overwhelm him. If he is angry at root level because it seems to him that his father always criticized, rather than complimenting and affirming him, he will feel rage at his boss's corrections but self-defensively stifle his stormy response until at home he can "thunder and lightning" all over his family. If confronted about this behavior, he projects his guilt onto everyone else and withdraws into a far corner of the house to pout, punching a hole in the wall as he leaves the room.

4. Manipulative

He has a tendency to manipulate others and to exploit flaws and weaknesses in them. For example: George knew that his wife, Virginia, was unhealed in her relation to her father, who had wounded her with harsh criticism and near total lack of affection when she was a child. Because of her judgments and expectations, she found it almost impossible to discipline either her emotions or her tongue when she perceived that she was being rejected or accused again by others. Day after day George would come home from work, say little or nothing to her in greeting, and then make some snide remark about her choice of menus as he filled his dinner plate on his way to the TV to eat in isolation from the rest of the family. There he would remain, transfixed until after the evening news, whereupon he expected to be met by a warm and willing sex partner. Virginia tried to control her anger, but when irritation would grow to the point that she finally exploded in ugly, uncontrollable tirades, George would use her verbal attacks as his *excuse* not to share with her. And then he would relate, sometimes with tears, his poor-abused-husband tale of woe to anyone who would listen.

Friends and prayer ministers attempted to make both George and

Virginia aware of the destructive dynamic going on between the two of them and tried to minister healing to them. Prayers were offered, and practical advice and supportive encouragement for self-discipline were given. But George *needed* to set Virginia up to attack him in order to maintain his right to hide in the fortress he had built from childhood to insure protection from the destructive onslaught of "mother."

5. Cannot relate corporately

The typical molester never learned to relate corporately. His parents' relationship to each other may have been marked by alcoholism, wife beating, death, divorce, frequent separations, physical disabilities, mental illness, or family stress. Not only were his parents isolated from each other and he from them, but he also did not feel close to brothers and sisters. There was no one in whom he could confide within the family.[17] He fears intimacy, because to him it means loss of control and vulnerability to the destructive imperfections of others. He chooses the familiar agony of loneliness rather than risking the unpredictable kinds and measures of pain he is certain lurk "poised to get him" from the world beyond his defenses.

6. Immature

He avoids efforts necessary for real growth and thus remains immature. His relationships are all of a secondary nature. He may belong to many organizations. He may even be a working member of a prayer group or home fellowship group in the church. But no one is allowed to *know* him. Rather than invest himself with people heart to heart, sharing, learning, and growing together *with* them; carrying others' burdens as if they were his own; and letting others see and minister to his spirit's needs, he relates superficially. He may be numbered *on* a team, playing according to the rules of the game but unable to experience what it is to *be* part of a team, moving in one accord with others, sensing what is needed in the way of give and take, advance and retreat, to accomplish corporate victory.

He may be keenly aware of his own inadequacies but cannot seek any kind of counsel for fear of discovery. He is afraid to ask questions because he thinks he is expected to have the answers. Though he may feel guilty for transgressions, he is terrified to confess. He doesn't know that he is loved just as he is, that sins are forgivable, and that most people learn more by their mistakes than by their successes. Because of fear and unwillingness to forgive those who wounded him from childhood, he has little ability to believe that others could have compassion on him and grant him forgiveness. So he exists in tension, laboring constantly to preserve his façade, tired and angry, often subject to periods of depression.

7. Need to punish

A molester may be burdened with a tremendous need to punish. If he hated his mother, he may be fueled by a powerful propensity to take revenge by defiling women. A young Christian father came to us years ago, horrified that he had succumbed to the temptation to sexually fondle his three-year-old daughter. It was a first violation, and he had caught himself before going very far. "How could I have done such a thing?" he asked, through tears.

As we ministered to him, he confessed with great shame several instances of voyeurism. When we pursued his family history, he resisted, declaring that he had been raised by good people who truly cared for him. He couldn't believe that he could possibly hold any animosity, especially toward his mother, whom he remembered as a very "sweet" person. As we visited further, he made repeated references to the "sweetness" of his mother. When we asked specific questions concerning the way his sweet mother disciplined him, we discovered that she had controlled him by sweet manipulations that put him under guilt. "Darling, sweetheart, you don't *want* to do that. You'll make Mother feel bad. You don't want to *hurt* Mother, do you? Mother *loves* you so." As a matter a fact, he *did* want to do the thing she wanted him to quit doing. But somehow he never felt free to do what he wanted or to express his true feelings about anything. He was laboring under what we call "parental inversion." (See chapter 2 of our book *Letting Go of*

Your Past.) He was a parent to his parent. He didn't dare feel anything that would "make" Mom feel bad, for she had made him responsible to "make" her feel good. Sometimes he felt like he was drowning in a stream of warm maple syrup, and there was no way to get clear of the sticky stuff. But he couldn't admit even to himself that he held strong negative feelings toward his lovely, fragile parent who loved him so intensely.

Suppressed animosity festered inside his heart, unconfessed for years, before it finally began to manifest as perverted curiosity and twisted affection rising to defile "woman." Why was he drawn to defile a child? Why not a mature woman who would seem to more adequately represent his mother figure? Because with an adult female he felt over-powered and helpless. With a child he could feel in control.

8. No self-discipline

A sexual abuser has no strength of spirit for self-discipline. Strength of spirit is built on basic trust and is prerequisite to being able to say yes and no from one's own center of decision. Such strength is essential if a person is to be able to stand and walk according to the decisions he has made, regardless of pressure in his circumstances. Strength of spirit is developed as one is nurtured by unconditional love and affection from parents, as we receive and interrelate with others, and as we mature in a vital relationship to Father God. But an abuser, having no well of spiritual strength, depends on strength of flesh and willpower, which fail him. He develops *private* practices to *comfort* himself in *isolation*:

- Masturbation becomes identified with comfort and release in safe solitude. It provides him with a momen-tary sense of well-being. If he practices this long enough, it may become addictive, a track to run on. In the absence of wholesome nurturing relationships with others, he has become less and less able to experience *corporately*. This inability expresses more dramatically in sex than in any other area of his life because of fear of vulnerability in intimacy. He learns more and more to identify his sexuality with his *own genital pleasure* rather than in *meeting* another person with his *entire being*. Sexual intercourse for him becomes nothing more than masturbation in the woman's embrace. He cannot be a true lover.

• He occupies himself with private hobbies, endless distractions, and pleasures that are self-gratifying.

• He involves himself with much busyness that excludes participation with others.

• Drugs and/or alcohol may become a serious problem. As many as one out of three molesters are substance abusers.[18] Other addictions such as smoking and/or overeating can also become a serious problem as they become identified as that which dulls pain.

• Sexual encounters—like drugs, alcohol, and overeating— are sought after to satisfy a deep need for comfort, feeding, and healing in relationship. Since superficial sexual experiences cannot reach deep needs but only titillate, the encounters themselves create additional hunger and vulnerability to temptation.

Suppose the potential molester accepts the Lord. Rather than relate to the *person* of the Lord, he relates only to the laws, forms, rules, regulations, theologies, and liturgies *about* the Lord.

Suppose the potential molester marries. He relates to his wife from a possessive and demanding bargaining base out of a need to control and be fulfilled (or passively submits to his wife) rather than sharing with her and blessing her.

Love and nurture are available from both sources (even though he tends to marry a wife who will fulfill his judgments).

Because of his strong desire to win, to succeed, to be right, and to be well thought of, his life is characterized by defensiveness and *striving*, which become a prison for his hardened heart. Very little love or nurture penetrates to melt his heart of stone. Therefore, he loses the capacity to identify properly or to sort and coordinate objectively the realities of thought and emotion within his heart. He also has difficulty integrating new experience; thus he fails to grow.

He hungers for belonging and intimacy, which he cannot put into words. He has little or no experience in filling his needs in healthy ways; indeed, he is not even aware of what he truly needs.[19] Suppression of natural emotions and desires produces increasing desperation. The misery of loneliness, fear of vulnerability, and failure cause him to seek affirmation and love from his wife. But as a lover, he functions like a vacuum cleaner. Since he does not know how to need, he demands. She feels drained as he gives almost nothing of himself. As I said earlier, sex with his wife has a quality of masturbation. He caresses her, but it is for his gratification; he is unaware that it is not for her sake. Gradually his wife withdraws from him, feeling both used and depleted. That reinforces the feelings of rejection that have always existed in him, and he finds it increasingly difficult to approach her. He has always enjoyed playing the hero figure around young girls with whom he feels less threatened than he does in the presence of his wife or other mature females. He flirts with the babysitter and makes off-color remarks that reflect a "teeny-bopper" mentality toward sex. His wife may be overworked, grieved, and in need of comfort, but he ignores her in order to "help" a neighbor lady in distress. The rest of the time, he may go hunting or fishing alone, anything to escape his wife.[20] Pornography may be his favorite reading material, but he tries to keep it undercover.

When his own child reaches out to him for attention and father love, he feels chosen, needed, and loved, but he responds out of his immaturity and sickness. He embraces his daughter, having no intention at first to violate her. But suppressed emotions and desires flood up in confusion; he runs on his *practiced track of self-gratification* (as with masturbation) and is swept into molestation and incest.

Horrified, he scrambles to protect himself by offering frantic excuses for his behavior: "I love you so much. I couldn't help myself." "Daddy is so lonely. Mommy doesn't love him anymore." He may threaten the victim physically if she tells or frighten her by talking about the destructive consequences she could cause in the whole family. "This will have to be our secret."

If he has any real sense of guilt, he is incapable of dealing with it. He has never truly forgiven those who wounded and/or abused him in his own childhood; now his present feelings trigger into ancient ones that powerfully fuel his inability to forgive himself for similar abusive acts. His practiced condemnation of others turns crushingly inward to afflict himself, and fear of discovery looms monstrously before him.

If he has any thoughts of seeking help, those are fleeting because of his long-standing mistrust of authority, augmented now by a paralyzing fear of the consequences of discovery. His mind races to rationalize and shorts out, and he sinks deeply into suppression of guilt and perhaps even of conscious memory. Pressure inside of him increases in proportion to the weight of the suppression. An overwhelming need for comfort then overcomes him, and he succumbs to the temptation to repeat his acts of violation. Repetition has an increasingly powerful numbing effect on conscience.

When the abuser's offenses are discovered, his reactions are likely to be any or all of these, in sequence:

Denial

The abuser may proclaim his innocence in the same way that a small child frantically insists, "I didn't do it! I didn't do it! I didn't! Somebody's lying to get me in trouble!" when the evidence is clearly before him and his accusers. His denial speaks of an immature and irrational belief that if he says "not guilty" loud enough and long enough, someone is bound to believe him and "let him off the hook."

Denial may also reflect his suppression of conscious memory and therefore his unawareness of guilt. At least in that moment, he may actually believe what he is saying.

Minimization of the seriousness of the offense

The abuser may insist, "Well, I touched her, but only a few times. It isn't like she was raped. She'll get over it." Or, "We were just playing around—you know—just wrestling, having fun. I was tickling her. It was only an accident."

Or he may admit to having approached his daughter to molest her and say, "I don't know why I did it. But it was only a couple of times, and I'm sorry. I didn't mean to hurt her, and it won't ever happen again. I can make it up to her." If put into words, the prevailing attitude is, "There—now I've said it. It's over with. Let's go on to other matters."

Rationalization

Rationalization is sometimes offered in the form of fragile excuses, "I couldn't help myself," "I was under such pressure," "I was so lonely," and so on. But often his way of rationalizing is much more deceptive and subtle. The story of Bill, Linda, and Karen in chapter 1 provides us with an excellent example. Let us add a few details to that account.

One might have questioned, "Why did Bill fall into his old patterns of irritability and temper when his relationship with Linda seemed to be going so well? Did it happen only because he tried to sustain his healing without further counsel or the encouragement of a support group?

The answer to both of those questions is the same. Bill could not sustain his healing, nor could he continue in close relationship with people who could discern and objectively see through his role-playing, because he was living under increasing pressure to hide his sin.

Soon after Bill's return home, Karen had mentioned to her mother that her father's behavior toward her had been inappropriate. Linda had immediately talked to him about it, and he had responded rather woundedly, denying any kind of violation, accompanied by a very plausible-sounding fabrication concerning what had happened that

"Karen must have misinterpreted." Linda wanted to believe him, and when she reported to Karen what her father had said, Karen answered with a puzzled, "Well, I guess, maybe..." and was afraid to press the issue.

Bill was relieved—on the surface. The subject had been broached. He had lied about it and had been believed. He told himself that the past was past, and he felt justified by the thought, "I won't do it again." He *rationalized*, "If I had admitted my guilt, it would have hurt every-body—Linda, my parents and in-laws, the other kids, my friends, church—even Karen. She still needs a father. I can make it all up to them." Bill's rationalization was like an alcoholic's justification for "one more drink."

He seemed to be doing well for nearly a year, and then everything came crashing in on him, double trouble for a lie. When the truth was revealed and he was put out of the house, he left protesting frantically, "I didn't do it!" Later he officially admitted to a "once or twice" offense. Privately to Linda he confessed to "three or four times." Before filing for divorce, she called him to say, "I don't want to end this marriage on the basis of a confession of 'three or four times.' Who is telling the truth—you or Karen?" His response was short: "You'd better listen to your daughter."

Accusation

Often an abuser rationalizes to the point of accusing his victim of seduction. "She made me do it." "I didn't want to, but I couldn't help myself." He may abuse her with name-calling: "Tramp!" "Whore!" Frequently when he begins to experience his world crumbling around him, he places the blame on the victim: "I've lost everything because of you." Some time later he may come to his senses and reach a true and balanced perspective in which he sees that he is reaping for his own sin, but the damage has been done. As I said earlier, a victim of sexual abuse usually tends, on her own, to assume inappropriate guilt; his accusations help to confirm that to her troubled heart.

The abuser may tumble around for quite a while in a confusion of unreality, fear, anger, remorse, and self-pity before he arrives at real repentance. He must be separated from the possibility of repeated encounters until in-depth prayer ministry has dealt sufficiently with *causes* and he has brought forth "*fruit in keeping with repentance*" (Matt. 3:8, emphasis added; see also Acts 26:20).

To say that one is sorry, even with tears, is not necessarily to be repentant. A person may be sorry that he has failed to be what he wanted to be, sorry that he was caught, sorry for his *own* loss and pain. Real repentance happens when a person becomes sorry for the pain and loss his sin has cost another. He is wounded and grieved for *their* sake. It means a change of heart and a right about-face in motivation, attitude, and action.

Such change is not accomplished overnight. The abuser's old way must be brought to death on the cross. "Every tree therefore that does not bear good fruit is cut down and thrown into the fire" (Matt. 3:10). A new way must be built into him, a new tree of life. Fruit does not appear immediately on a new tree. Too often the church has rushed in to pronounce that an abuser is repentant when his new tree has begun to put forth only leaves.

The abuser must be separated from his family as long as it takes for change. Depending on the laws of the state, prosecution and imprisonment may be inevitable. But imprisonment will not deter him from future violations. From the church he needs:

- Unconditional love and confrontation in love
- Compassion and forgiveness
- The support of friendship
- Intercessory prayer

From qualified prayer ministers he needs adequate counsel, which includes:

- Full confession of his present sins (James 5:16). This should include asking forgiveness from the victim, the family, and others who have been injured by his actions. It should also include a clear message to the victim that he assumes full responsibility for the molestations. She is not the guilty one.

- Discovery of the root causes for his problems (Luke 6:43–45; Eph. 5:13; Heb. 12:15)

- Choosing to forgive those who wounded him from child-hood on (Matt. 6:14–15)

- Repentance for his reaction to those hurts, asking forgiveness for his responses

- Assurances of forgiveness (John 20:23; 1 John 1:9)

- Prayers (aloud, with him) for the healing of his own wounded spirit (2 Cor. 1:1–6)

- Prayers (aloud, with him) for the creation of a new and right spirit within him (Ps. 51:10; Ezek. 36:26)

- Prayers (aloud, with him) for the bringing to death of the old habit structures in the "old man" (Rom. 8:13; Eph. 4:22; Col. 3:3–9)

- Discipline to walk in the new way (Rom. 6:11–14; 2 Tim. 1:7)

- Teaching concerning the laws of God, the sanctity of marriage, the holiness of sex, the functions of a father's love, the blessings of self-sacrifice, the meaning of corpo-rateness, and the like

- Prayers that the Lord will set him free to receive teaching and nurture that he may grow up inside to become a mature man

- Discernment on the part of the prayer minister to determine when the abuser has come to real repentance and is capable of living a new life that produces the fruit of repentance season after season

It seems to me that the reaction of the majority of people to the abuser of little children is one of horror, disgust, and often hate. Often people unknowingly project their own unconfessed guilt onto such a one whose sin is so obvious and punish it there.

As Christians we need to recognize the seriousness of his offense:

It would be better for him if a millstone were hung around his neck and he were thrown into the sea, than that he should cause one of these little ones to stumble.

—Luke 17:2

At the same time we need to remember that we are dealing with one who wounded others because of his own woundedness. He needs to be disciplined not as an object of our vengeance but for his good: "He [God] disciplines us for our good, that we may share His holiness" (Heb. 12:10).

The abuser needs to be hauled to account and made to suffer enough of the consequences of his actions to write lessons on his heart. As Christians we are called not only to rebuke the brother who sins but also to *forgive* him (Luke 17:3). We must examine our own hearts to see to it that as we pronounce judgment, administer sentencing, or serve in prayer ministry, our motivations are in tune with the motivations of God.

Or do you think lightly of the riches of His kindness and forbearance and patience, not knowing that the kindness of God leads you to repentance?

—ROMANS 2:4

Godly kindness does not look the other way, nor does it make excuses. In kindness God loves the sinner, while He, directly and through human authorities, deals with his sin.

Chapter 7

TROUBLE AND HEALING IN THE FAMILY

Let each individual among you also love his own wife even as himself; and let the wife see to it that she respect her husband.

EPHESIANS 5:33

And, fathers, do not provoke your children to anger; but bring them up in the discipline and instruction of the Lord.

EPHESIANS 6:4

WHEN A HUSBAND OR FATHER IS DISCOVERED TO BE A SEXUAL abuser, especially if he violated his own child, the entire family is victimized. Foundations crumble, hopes and dreams vanish, loyalties are thrown into conflict, emotions go crazy, and faith is put to extreme test.

Because we are one body in Christ, and "if one member suffers, all the members suffer with it" (1 Cor. 12:26), not only those in the abuser's immediate family but also everyone in the extended family and the church family share the burden of pain and confusion. They sense the heaviness of it, inwardly wrestle with it, pray about it, and long to make some kind of helpful response. But too seldom are they sufficiently aware of what the abuser's wife and children are feeling so as to be able to say appropriately and effectively, "I know what you are going through, and I want you to know that I am standing with you, available for whatever needs I can fill."

Recently I visited with Linda and her two boys, who are still in our community and well into the redemptive process following the breakup of their family after it was discovered that Bill had been molesting Karen. (See chapter 1.) My question to Linda was, "Can you tell me what you've been through? Can you share what you have felt?"

I will not elaborate on her words but rather trust that the Lord will enable the reader to empathize with the simplicity and straightforwardness of her testimony. She said:

> When I found out what Bill had done, I felt like I was caught in a complicated web. It was so unbelievable—so tremendously big I couldn't comprehend it! I was in shock. I went through the motions of doing what I knew I had to do. I put him out.
>
> At first I thought, "Bill's sin is against Karen, not me." But several weeks later reality sank in—
>
> The sick lies he told me—the deception—
>
> It all hit me like a BRICK! Trust was shattered. The past six years had been a lie!
>
> I WAS ANGRY!
>
> I felt like a patsy—gullible—betrayed.
>
> It hit my mother-bear instinct. I should have been there to see, to protect, to react. But I'd failed.
>
> I was angry at myself for being so blind and trusting.
>
> I was so confused. Bill's and Karen's stories were so conflicting. Her *actions* said he did it. He *said* he didn't. But I *knew* she was telling the truth.
>
> I had to face my anger; let it live. So I banged on pillows, dragging out years of swallowed anger—expressing it and feeling it.
>
> And all the while Karen was treating me like the villain, continuing to punish me.

She said, "You should have known. I shouldn't have had to tell you!!"

I wondered, "Can I really say I didn't see?"

I could remember.

Bill's playing around, grabbing her in a hug—

Like he'd always done with the kids. But then—

Sometimes he'd touch her breast.

I'd say, "Watch out. You have to be careful. She's budding now."

He'd stop and say, "Oh, yeah." I'd have a little sinking feeling, but...

It was so hard for me, wanting so badly to repair the damage for my daughter, but she was pushing me away!

I had to face some mixed feelings about her too: I loved her so much. But I had to deal with my anger.

She had become "the other woman." She had aced me out just by "being"!

Mostly I was angry that something could go on so long.

Through my decision to marry Bill, I had blown my whole life!—No control! Nobody told me—I felt betrayed on all sides—helplessness.

Loneliness overwhelmed me for a while, and I was blown away, looking for security—somebody who'd tell me everything will be OK.

I was so vulnerable—and had such a lack of discernment— so shattered—no confidence at all in my ability to see—I really lost it for a while.

I had a crush on my counselor. He said we were mutually attracted, but he wasn't available.

There was a string of others—all authority figures—who wanted to be available.

Absolutely everything in my life was shaken to the roots and had to be built again—moral structures and everything, especially since I hadn't really completed my own individuation before I was married.

For a while my boys were putting a lot of pressure on Bill and me to "kiss and make up." Joey would still like that. But Matt understands. Joey's younger, and he just loves his daddy and can't understand why Mommy doesn't.

I've been in a bind. I could tell the boys the truth and destroy the image of their father, or I could be the bad guy.

I decided I'd help them to face the facts, not elaborating, not minimizing.

So when Bill wasn't paying child support or paying his bills, and he was feeding the kids a line about how I had all his money, I laid out the facts. But I told them their daddy was sick, that his actions were not deliberate, that he was not a bad guy, that he needs help and healing.

Matt has been very angry, defensive, fiercely loyal to his father, and parentally inverted. He tries to be a father to his father and sticks up for him whenever anyone says anything negative about him.

Both of the boys want so much to believe that when Bill says sorry, he really means it.

I can forgive Bill. But I can't be a wife to him again. Trust and respect are gone.

Matt (age thirteen) wanted to tell how he felt, "if it would help some other kid." But he wanted to be asked specific questions:

"What was your reaction when you first heard about what your dad had done?"

"I didn't believe it. I said, 'I don't care. My dad wouldn't have done anything like that.'"

"What made you believe it?"

"The evidence. The separation. The court. He confessed."

"How did that make you feel, Matt?"

"Like glass—shattered! Respect—dependability...but it didn't even seem real—more like a nightmare you'd like to wake up from."

"How did you feel when he had to go to jail?"

"Sorry for him. That he wouldn't have a life. No freedom. No fun."

"Do you believe the jail will do him any good?"

"Yeah. Maybe it'll make him grow up, give him time to think, help him separate fact from fantasy. He has to go to a counselor."

"What is the most important message that you would like to send to your dad?"

"That I'll always love him, no matter what."

"What is the best wish that you would make for him, the most important prayer that you would say for him?"

"That he could grow up."

"Sometimes you're awfully angry. Who are you angry with?"

"My dad."

"Are you angry at Karen?"

"No, she didn't do anything. Dad did it to her."

"Are you angry with your mom?"

"Well—you know how you get angry with moms!" He laughed. "But I'm not angry with her about—you know—I don't blame her."

"Matt, you've had trouble sleeping. Why is that?"

"I keep thinking about my dad. About the fun things I'd like to do with him."

"Do you worry about how other people feel about your dad?"

"I don't want him to lose friends. I don't want people to not like him or think he's a weirdo."

"How's Joey doing?"

"He thinks the judge was mean to put dad in jail. He just wants to be with him."

"Does Joey kind of look to you as a dad now?"

"*I am his dad!*"

Linda smiled appreciatively and tenderly. "Matt, you have uncles and grandparents. Let them be dads. You just keep on doing a super job of being a big brother."

I watched big brother in operation one day not long ago. He was supervising the writing of Joey's letter to their dad. Joey sat with pencil poised, staring off into space. Matt tried to hurry him, and Joey objected, "I'm thinking!"

"You don't have to think. Just write, 'Dear Dad, I love you.'"

Joey started, wrote a word or two, and spaced out again.

"Come on, Joey—keep going—keep going."

Finally Joey's letter was completed: "Dear Dad, I love you. I am sad for you."

The only adverb Joey could think of for that night's homework assignment was "sadly." But Matt will be there to keep him going. And God, Linda, the rest of the family, and the church are faithfully and lovingly there to keep Matt going and to see that he has some time just to be a kid.

This is a family moving ahead in the Lord's healing process. Despite substantial difficulties, new life is opening beautifully before them. They have made choices to forgive and to love unconditionally, despite their sometimes screaming feelings, "I could kill him!" And the Lord has caused those repeated choices to become a reality that opens doors to continued healing and blessing.

> And in the same way the Spirit also helps our weakness; for we do not know how to pray as we should, but the Spirit Himself intercedes for us with groanings too deep for words; and He who searches the hearts knows what the mind of the Spirit is, because He intercedes for the saints according to the will of God. And we know that God causes all things to work together for good to those who love God, to those who are called according to His purpose.
>
> —Romans 8:26–28

Many families are not so blessed with recuperative sources as this family. Many fall apart, seemingly irrevocably. We call the church to be aware, prepared, and available as the healing body it was created to be.

Appendix of Scriptures

The Loving Nature of Father God

Although my father and my mother have forsaken me, yet the Lord will take me up [adopt me as His child].

—Psalm 27:10, amp

God is our refuge and strength, a very present help in trouble.

—Psalm 46:1

Give thanks to the Lord, for He is good; for His lovingkindness is everlasting.

—Psalm 118:1

The Lord is for me; I will not fear; what can man do to me?

—Psalm 118:6

For God so loved the world, that He gave His only begotten Son, that whoever believes in Him should not perish, but have eternal life.

—John 3:16

Let not your heart be troubled; believe in God, believe also in Me. In My Father's house are many dwelling places; if it were not so, I would have told you; for I go to prepare a place for you.

—John 14:1–2

We know that God causes all things to work together for good to those who love God, to those who are called according to His purpose.

—Romans 8:28

Blessed be the God and Father of our Lord Jesus Christ, the Father of mercies and God of all comfort; who comforts us in all our affliction so that we may be able to comfort those who are in any affliction with the comfort with which we ourselves are comforted by God.

—2 Corinthians 1:3–4

God, being rich in mercy, because of His great love with which He loved us, even when we were dead in our transgressions, made us alive together with Christ (by grace you have been saved), and raised us up with Him in the heavenly places, in Christ Jesus.

—Ephesians 2:5–6

The Lord is not slow about His promise, as some count slowness, but is patient toward you, not wishing for any to perish but for all to come to repentance.

—2 Peter 3:9

And we have come to know and have believed the love which God has for us. God is love, and the one who abides in love abides in God, and God abides in him.

—1 John 4:16

We love, because He first loved us.

—1 John 4:19

FORGIVENESS

But there is forgiveness with Thee, that Thou mayest be feared.
—PSALM 130:4

And forgive us our debts, as we also have forgiven our debtors.
—MATTHEW 6:12

For if you forgive men for their transgressions, your heavenly Father will also forgive you. But if you do not forgive men, then your Father will not forgive your transgressions.
—MATTHEW 6:14–15

And whenever you stand praying, forgive, if you have anything against anyone; so that your Father also who is in heaven may forgive you your transgressions. But if you do not forgive, neither will your Father who is in heaven forgive your transgressions.
—MARK 11:25–26

Be on your guard! If your brother sins, rebuke him; and if he repents, forgive him. And if he sins against you seven times a day, and returns to you seven times, saying, "I repent," forgive him.
—LUKE 17:3–4

The God of our fathers raised up Jesus.... He is the one whom God exalted to His right hand as a Prince and a Savior, to grant repentance...and forgiveness of sins.
—ACTS 5:30–31

In Him we have redemption through His blood, the forgiveness of our trespasses, according to the riches of His grace, which He lavished upon us.
—EPHESIANS 1:7–8

Let all bitterness and wrath and anger and clamor and slander be put away from you, along with all malice, and be kind to one another, tender-hearted, forgiving each other, just as God in Christ also has forgiven you.

—EPHESIANS 4:31–32

And so, as those who have been chosen of God, holy and beloved, put on a heart of compassion, kindness, humility, gentleness and patience; bearing with one another, and forgiving each other, whoever has a complaint against anyone; just as the Lord forgave you, so also should you.

—COLOSSIANS 3:12–13

If we confess our sins, He is faithful and righteous to forgive us our sins and to cleanse us from all unrighteousness. If we say we have not sinned, we make Him a liar, and His word is not in us.

—1 JOHN 1:9–10

PARDON

...who pardons all your iniquities; who heals all your diseases; who redeems your life from the pit; who crowns you with lovingkindness and compassion.

—PSALM 103:3–4

I, even I, am the one who wipes out your transgressions for My own sake; and I will not remember your sins.

—ISAIAH 43:25

Let the wicked forsake his way, and the unrighteous man his thoughts; and let him return to the LORD, and He will have compassion on him; and to our God, for He will abundantly pardon.

—ISAIAH 55:7

REMISSION OF SINS

As far as the east is from the west, so far has He removed our transgressions from us.

—PSALM 103:12

For this is My blood of the covenant, which is poured out for many for forgiveness of sins.

—MATTHEW 26:28

And he came into all the district around the Jordan, preaching a baptism of repentance for the forgiveness of sins.

—LUKE 3:3

And He said to them, "Thus it is written, that the Christ should suffer and rise again from the dead on the third day; and that repentance for forgiveness of sins should be proclaimed in His name to all the nations, beginning from Jerusalem."

—LUKE 24:46–47

Repent therefore and return, that your sins may be wiped away, in order that times of refreshing may come from the presence of the Lord; and that He may send Jesus, the Christ appointed for you.

—ACTS 3:19

COMPASSION AND MERCY

Just as a father has compassion on his children, so the LORD has compassion on those who fear Him.

—PSALM 103:13

But the lovingkindness of the LORD is from everlasting to everlasting on those who fear Him, and His righteousness to children's children.

—PSALM 103:17

Do not let kindness and truth leave you; bind them about your neck, write them on the tablet of your heart.

—PROVERBS 3:3

The LORD's lovingkindnesses indeed never cease, for His compassions never fail.

—LAMENTATIONS 3:22

"Yet even now," declares the LORD, "return to Me with all your heart, and with fasting, weeping, and mourning; and rend your heart and not your garments." Now return to the LORD your God, for He is gracious and compassionate, slow to anger, abounding in lovingkindness, and relenting of evil.

—JOEL 2:12–13

He has told you, O man, what is good; and what does the LORD require of you but to do justice, to love kindness, and to walk humbly with your God?

—MICAH 6:8

Blessed are the merciful, for they shall receive mercy.

—MATTHEW 5:7

Be merciful, just as your Father is merciful.

—LUKE 6:36

He saved us, not on the basis of deeds which we have done in righteousness, but according to His mercy, by the washing of regeneration and renewing by the Holy Spirit, whom He poured out upon us richly through Jesus Christ our Savior, that being justified by His grace we might be made heirs according to the hope of eternal life.

—Titus 3:5-7

Peace, Sleep, and Rest in the Lord

My presence shall go with you, and I will give you rest.

—Exodus 33:14

I lay down and slept; I awoke, for the Lord sustains me.

—Psalm 3:5

In peace I will both lie down and sleep, for Thou alone, O Lord, dost make me to dwell in safety.

—Psalm 4:8

The Lord will give strength to His people; the Lord will bless His people with peace.

—Psalm 29:11

Return to your rest, O my soul, for the Lord has dealt bountifully with you.

—Psalm 116:7

I will lift up my eyes to the mountains:
From whence shall my help come?
My help comes from the Lord,
Who made heaven and earth.
He will not allow your foot to slip;
He who keeps you will not slumber.
Behold, He who keeps Israel
Will neither slumber nor sleep.
The Lord is your keeper;
The Lord is your shade on your right hand.

The sun will not smite you by day, nor the moon by night.
The LORD will protect you from all evil;
He will keep your soul.
The LORD will guard your going out and your coming in
From this time forth and forever.

—PSALM 121

For He gives to His beloved even in his sleep.

—PSALM 127:2

Surely I have composed and quieted my soul;
Like a weaned child rests against his mother,
My soul is like a weaned child within me.
…hope in the LORD
From this time forth and forever.

—PSALM 131:2–3

The steadfast of mind Thou wilt keep in perfect peace, because he trusts in Thee.

—ISAIAH 26:3

For I [the Lord] satisfy the weary ones and refresh everyone who languishes.

—JEREMIAH 31:25

Take My yoke upon you, and learn from Me, for I am gentle and humble in heart; and you shall find rest for your souls.

—MATTHEW 11:29

Let not your heart be troubled; believe in God, believe also in Me.

—JOHN 14:1

Peace I leave with you; My peace I give to you; not as the world gives, do I give to you. Let not your heart be troubled, nor let it be fearful.

—John 14:27

And the peace of God, which surpasses all comprehension, shall guard your hearts and your minds in Christ Jesus.

—Philippians 4:7

I can do all things through Him who strengthens me.

—Philippians 4:13

Notes

Introduction

1. David B. Peters, *A Betrayal of Innocence* (Nashville: Word Publishing, 1986), 19–20.

Chapter 1
Eyes to See and Ears to Hear

1. Steven L. Shearer, PhD, and Carol A. Herbert, MD, "Long-Term Effects of Unresolved Sexual Trauma," *American Family Physician* 36, no. 4 (October 1987): 170.

Chapter 2
The Depths of Devastation

1. Amy Carmichael, *If* (Fort Washington, PA: CLC Publications, 1992).

Chapter 3
Suppression, Regression, and Frigidity

1. Biblos.com, "Strong's number 2266, *chabar*" Strong's Numbers Online Dictionary, http://strongsnumbers.com/hebrew/2266.htm (accessed March 23, 2009).
2. Shearer and Herbert, "Long-Term Effects of Unresolved Sexual Trauma," 170, 174.

Chapter 4
A Garland for Ashes—the Healing Process

1. Shearer and Herbert, "Long-Term Effects of Unresolved Sexual Trauma," 173–174.
2. J. L. Herman and L. Hirschman, *Father-Daughter Incest* (Cambridge, MA: Harvard University Press, 1981).

Chapter 5
"Ministry" That Devours the Afflicted

1. Peters, *A Betrayal of Innocence*, 97–98. Italics have been added for emphasis.

2. Special Report, "How Common Is Pastoral Indiscretion?" *Leadership*, Winter 1988, 12–13.

Chapter 6
The Characteristics of an Abuser

1. Peters, *A Betrayal of Innocence*, 21.

2. National Clearinghouse on Family Violence, "Adolescent Sex Offenders," http://www.phac-aspc.gc.ca/ncfv-cnivf/familyviolence/html/ nfntsxadolinfractions_e.html (accessed January 30, 2009), 3.

3. Adam M. Tomison, "Update on Child Sexual Abuse," National Child Protection Clearinghouse, *Issues in Child Abuse Prevention* 5, Summer 1995, http://www.aifs.gov.au/nch/pubs/issues/issues5/issues5.html (accessed January 29, 2009), 1.

4. Dorothy M. Neddermeyer, PhD, "Sex Offender Profile," Ezine Articles, http://ezinearticles.com/?Sex-Offender-Profile&id=133344 (accessed March 25, 2009), 1–2.

5. William E. Prendergast, PhD, *Treating Sex Offenders in Correctional Institutions and Outpatient Clinics* (New York: The Haworth Press, 1991), 11.

6. Ibid., 41.

7. Anne L. Horton, Barry L. Johnson, Lynn M. Roundy, and Doran Williams, *The Incest Perpetrator: A Family Member No One Wants to Treat* (Newbury Park, CA: Sage Publications, 1990), 80.

8. Prendergast, *Treating Sex Offenders in Correctional Institutions and Outpatient Clinics*, 12.

9. Ibid., 16.

10. Ibid., 12.

11. Ibid., 70.

12. Ibid., 12.

13. Ibid., 79–80.

14. Ibid., 27.

15. Ibid., 17.

16. Ibid., 62.

17. Horton, Johnson, Roundy, and Williams, *The Incest Perpetrator: A Family Member No One Wants to Treat*, 78–79.

18. "Profile of a Typical Child Sexual Abuser," Notes for Child Sexual Abuse, http://www.uplink.com.au/lawlibrary/Documents/Docs/Doc19.html (accessed January 29, 2009).

19. Horton, Johnson, Roundy, and Williams, *The Incest Perpetrator: A Family Member No One Wants to Treat*, 75.

20. Ibid., 84.

Other Books by John Loren and Paula Sandford

A Comprehensive Guide to Deliverance and Inner Healing

Awakening the Slumbering Spirit

Choosing Forgiveness

Elijah Among Us

Healing for a Woman's Emotions

Healing the Nations

Prophets, Healers and the Emerging Church

Life Transformed

Restoring the Christian Family

The Elijah Task

The Transformation Series:
Transforming the Inner Man
God's Power to Change
Letting Go of Your Past
Growing Pains

Why Good People Mess Up

For further information, contact:

Elijah House, Inc.
317 N. Pines Road
Spokane Valley, WA 99206
Web site: www.elijahhouse.org

How to Build Happy, Healthy, Safe Families in Today's World

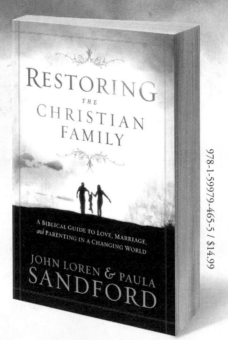

978-1-59979-465-5 / $14.99

Drawing from more than thirty years of counseling experience and providing honest and touching illustrations from their own family life, the Sandfords take you into the heart of the family. In *Restoring the Christian Family* they offer hope and healing to everyone who is struggling to keep their family together, happy, and whole.

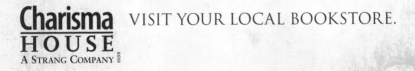

VISIT YOUR LOCAL BOOKSTORE.

FREE NEWSLETTERS

TO HELP EMPOWER YOUR LIFE

Why subscribe today?

☐ **DELIVERED DIRECTLY TO YOU.** All you have to do is open your inbox and read.

☐ **EXCLUSIVE CONTENT.** We cover the news overlooked by the mainstream press.

☐ **STAY CURRENT.** Find the latest court rulings, revivals, and cultural trends.

☐ **UPDATE OTHERS.** Easy to forward to friends and family with the click of your mouse.

CHOOSE THE E-NEWSLETTER THAT INTERESTS YOU MOST:

- Christian news
- Daily devotionals
- Spiritual empowerment
- And much, much more

SIGN UP AT: **http://freenewsletters.charismamag.com**

8178